To my husband, Joseph M. Puggelli

contents

acknowledgements

pr for people would not be complete unless I mention my complete gratitude to my husband, Joe Puggelli, for his superb work as an editor. Aside from being my partner, collaborator, and intellectual companion, this very talented and brilliant man is also the source for my continuing inspiration.

I also thank the many wonderful members of the press that I have had the privilege to work with during my long career.

I give thanks to my three children, David, Sarah and Katie for being the greatest joy of my life.

Finally, I thank all of my wonderful clients for giving me the opportunity to work with them to help them get the deserved recognition for who they are and what they do.

about this book

Patricia Vaccarino, founder of the Seattle-based boutique PR firm Xanthus Communications and its subsidiary *pr for people*, explains how professionals can build brand equity in their own names by implementing the 10Ps in *pr for people*. In an age of highly fragmented media, professionals need to differentiate themselves so they can communicate who they are and what they do. Ms. Vaccarino explains what individuals need to do to wage an effective public relations campaign during a time when everyone is clamoring to get heard.

"It is more challenging than ever for an author, a company, a product or an individual to break through the clutter and reach its target audiences because we are marketing in the age of fragmented media."

&. **Patricia Vaccarino**

"Good PR is establishing the greatest number of high quality relationships that reach across industries and sectors to get you a return on investment."

🐾 Patricia Vaccarino

introduction

people as brands.

Branding is not only meant for celebrities. We love celebrities and enjoy the beauty, intrigue and glamour that they bring to the world, but you can't count on celebrities to perform brain surgery, find a way to minimize bacterial infections, or give you sound financial advice to protect the future of your family and loved ones. Celebrities come and go. You are a professional and you are here to stay. You are accomplished, credentialed and smart. You have a real name. You don't act for a living. You work for a living. You have a real expertise that you have worked hard to cultivate. You have more to gain from developing your brand than any celebrity. It is more important than ever for you to build a strong brand identity, which is defined by who you are and what you do.

everyone must build a solid brand identity.

Now, in order to be seen and heard above the din and to reach the right target audiences, everyone must build a solid brand identity. All professionals, from every sector and industry, must build brand equity in their own names. Having a good professional reputation is obviously connected to establishing one's brand identity, but many people don't think strategically about how best to nurture this identity. Individuals have a need to build brand equity in their own names more than any company. Companies come and go through natural attrition or acquisition and merger, but an individual's professional name stays with him from the cradle to the grave. No matter what company a person is with, or what company a person will join in the future, individuals will always take their names and their reputations with them. Your brand is carefully crafted over time. It does not happen by accident. Your brand is the world's perception of who you are. The world's perception of who you are may differ from the reality of who you are, and to the world, this perception is reality. What we are dealing with is reality and perception. Perception is now the new reality. And it must be managed.

The story of how I decided to do *pr for people* deserves some mention. Back in the late 1990s, I had the pleasure to work with an Internet company called PublishingOnline. While I was there, I worked with individual authors who wanted to be published on the Internet. Some had never been published; some had been self-published; and some had been somewhat unhappily published by presses both small and large and wanted to take control over their own books and their careers. These authors were an eclectic group of intelligent individuals who all had talent and specific areas of expertise. I learned a lot from my experience at PublishingOnline and in particular I came to understand the needs of professionals who want to promote themselves as experts and who want to use their books as a tool to help grow their client base. I quickly learned there is a real need for professionals to market themselves the same as any company in a way that was cost effective and got results.

At PublishingOnline, although we published authors, we didn't have a standard promotion kit to help authors market their own books. We did what little we could do on a limited budget in the same manner of any other publishing house. Back then, our PR campaigns for people were simple:

- We promoted the person on our website.
- We sent out press releases to a short media list.
- We sent targeted email…which was a precursor of today what we would call a viral email marketing campaign.

Those tactics worked—then—but now times have changed dramatically. Today, those same tactics would simply fall flat and fail.

What is the difference between now and then? For one, the transition from the industrial age to the age of communication is complete. The media in all its forms is highly fragmented and becoming more so every day. The media is creating enormous clutter. You have probably heard of the term *clutter*. It's like a room full of people, who instead of taking turns to speak, everyone shouts at the top of their lungs at the same time. Now you must build a strong brand identity in order to be seen and heard above the din.

pr note

There is no single course of action that will help you to break through the clutter. **Breaking through the clutter requires a fully integrated and ongoing PR campaign.** All of the elements in your campaign must fit together in the same program, be implemented at the same time, and, most importantly, be sustained over an indefinite period of time.

We call these elements in the program the Ps in *pr for people*. By following the guidelines of *pr for people*, you stand a much greater chance to increase awareness for who you are and what you do **in a way that will help develop your career and increase your business.**

Have you ever wondered why there is so much clutter? It is media that is creating all the clutter. Many traditional media outlets are already dead or dying. Print newspapers seem to be disappearing altogether. Despite the high rate of failure, the media as an industry continues to be replenished with startup companies. Fifty to 100 new media outlets are added to the media space each business day. The numbers referring to media outlets include only newspapers, magazines, radio and television or cable programs and they do not include blogs, online media or social media websites. At last count, blog and social media tracker Technorati claims to have indexed 112.8 million blogs and over 250 million pieces of tagged social media. These numbers also do not include new social media outlets and the frequent addition of new users who are connecting on social networking websites such as Facebook, Linked-in and Twitter.

The expression "*break through the clutter*" has been used often. In fact, *break through the clutter* has become sort of a cliché. Among seasoned PR practitioners, *break through the clutter* was cited as a passé expression in the same vein as the following classic PR expressions: "*think outside the box*"; "*ROI,*" the acronym for *return on investment*; "*make it pop*"; and a "*fully integrated*" PR solution. In other words, in the PR world if you use any of these expressions you are no longer considered cool.

But I am not concerned so much with cool, or what's in and what's out, as I am with reality and certain truths that will always stand the test of time. The basic PR tenets in this book are the same now as they were ten years ago and they will be ten years from today. The fundamental principles governing PR never change. The vehicles used for promotion—types of media, new websites and technologies--will always change, but one thing will always remain the same: **Good PR is establishing the greatest number of high quality relationships that reach across industries and sectors to get you a return on investment.**

So I am going to return to those classic PR expressions and tell you why they are still critical to building your brand identity, which is defined by who you are and what you do.

break through the clutter.

To be successful in today's complex marketplace, you must be able to break through the clutter. It does not matter if you are an artist or an actor or an accountant or an attorney, you must have the ability to be seen and heard above the din. Breaking through the clutter requires dedication, persistence and hard work. I recently met a realtor at a networking group who told me that he was a source for *Seattle Magazine*, which means editors will go to him for information about the local real estate market and give him credit in the magazine. I told him not to stop there. Getting placed in only one publication is simply not enough to build sustained awareness for who you are and what you do. In today's business world, every professional must wage a campaign to seek placement in the full range of traditional media and social media outlets. Do all of your potential clients read or watch or listen to only one media outlet? Don't ever just stop at one. One media placement is only a starting point.

think outside the box.

How you define your brand should be precise, creative and memorable. You are not a celebrity. You are a professional with a job and a career or you are an entrepreneur with a business. Or maybe you are an up-and-coming actor, artist or singer—a creative talent—who wants fame. No matter what your occupation is, you must find a way to stand out from the crowd. I have a client who is a rabbi and is uniquely positioned as a youth and culture expert. I have a client who is a plastic surgeon, but he is not just a plastic surgeon: he is also an expert in the psychological aspects of cosmetic surgery. I have a beauty expert who knows everything there is to know about the conditioning and growth of naturally long eyelashes.

And while you must find a way to distinguish yourself from all the other professionals who share your same occupation, there is also a time when you must think inside the box. There is a time to simply say I am a rabbi, a physician or a beauty expert. Don't forget to think inside the box. But always remember when to shove that box aside and explode with an original or innovative idea that will get noticed!

roi.

Return on Investment is a term and a concept that will never go out of style. You must invest in yourself. You must invest in your own public relations campaign. Some people feel shy about self-promotion and believe that it is self-aggrandizing or even narcissistic. You must get over any reticence that tells you that by promoting yourself you are being immodest. This is business, not child's play. There is no room to be immature or clueless. To succeed in today's business environment, you must aggressively promote yourself and your business. You must embrace the fact that public relations or self-promotion is simply a business development tool and is necessary to grow your business and to increase revenue. You do not have the spectacular budget of a celebrity to work with, but you do have to have a budget. Your budget is what will dictate exactly how you can create your own fully integrated promotion and establish metrics to assess whether or not you did indeed get your return on your investment.

make it pop.

Your professional brand identity must be memorable. It's your name and now you are building a brand. Why does anyone want to do business with you? Why do they want to buy your book, your products or your services? Put yourself in the shoes of your potential clients. What are you going to offer them that no one else can offer in the same way? What distinguishes you from your competitors and elevates you to be a cut above the rest? Why would the press want to write about you or include your words in a feature article? Put yourself in the shoes of a reporter. What do you have to say that is timely, relevant and compelling?

No matter what expressions are deemed in or out, or what companies are considered market leaders, the challenge of promoting the individual has intensified. It will continue to intensify. There isn't going to be less clutter. In the next decade, there will be much more. For professionals to achieve business success at every level, a fully integrated PR campaign must be clever enough to outwit competitors and relevant enough to capture the attention of your community-of-interest. Your community-of-interest is everyone who stands to gain value from knowing you. One way to break through the clutter is to define who you are and what you do, and to be prepared to tell who you are and what you do in thirty seconds or less, especially when dealing with potential clients or the media. Even the editors of very small trade publications get 400 emails a day. In order to even be a contender among those 400 emails, you must be well prepared and well packaged, which means that you have to have a strong brand persona.

pr note

fully integrated pr solution.

To promote you, your brand, and your business, you must carefully plan all elements of your promotion, which include the following Ps of *pr for people*: Persona, Positioning, Perception, Platform, Planning, Press, Pitching, Partnering, Performance and Persistence. All of these pieces together help to create a brand identity where the whole is greater than the sum of its parts so that your message about who you are and what you do breaks through the clutter.

chapter one 🐾 persona

be human. your brand image.

Today's professionals need branding more than celebrities do because people who are experts have the power to make a profound and lasting impact on the world. They also need to make a living to support lifestyles, families and communities. Never before in history has the onus of responsibility placed on the shoulders of any one individual been so great. Every individual must work hard to demonstrate an ability to support a local community as well as the larger global community.

Who are you? What do you stand for? What are the main core attributes that differentiate you from other professionals who share your same occupation? There is no one else out there quite like you. Brand, in this case, is your persona.

There is no better time to reinvent and brand yourself than now. There is no stigma to making a change because a whole host of external factors are constantly forcing us all to change. Every individual has a unique set of skills and talents that can be adapted to a variety of industries.

Each of us has a unique cognitive profile that ultimately defines who we are, what we do, and maybe even how much money we make. The theory of multiple intelligences is more than educational jargon put forth by psychologists. In reality we all have varying degrees of intelligence: from creative intelligence and business intelligence to financial intelligence and social intelligence. Over forty types of intelligence have been identified and the list keeps growing. As you develop your brand persona, you need to think about the unique array of various types of intelligences that you possess.

As a professional you should not make the mistake of identifying yourself solely according to a job. Your affiliation with companies may come and go, but who you are and what you do should stand the test of time. This reality means you must clearly define your professional brand. It is more important than ever for you to take a stand to differentiate yourself from all others who share your same occupation.

To attract the right people, clients and partners, you must repel those people who would never be your clients and partners. You must take a stand and speak the truth about who you are. If you choose the middle road and describe yourself in an average way to avoid offending someone, know and understand that you have doomed your personal brand to mediocrity. By trying to offend no one, you have showed the world that you have nothing to offer to anyone.

The more clearly you define your name and your brand, the more you will simultaneously repel the wrong people and attract the right people. Repel people? Getting rid of the people who are all wrong for you and for your business may be the most cost effective and efficient decision you will ever make. Most people are too afraid to really differentiate themselves and will take a middle-of-the-road approach. Staying safely in the middle will waste your time and get you nowhere. Get rid of the wrong people. Define your name. Refine it further. Make it sharp. Don't be afraid of standing out. Exceptional people always scare the weak and mediocre.

what's in a name?

Let's start with your name. When someone mentions your name, what memories are conjured in the minds of your colleagues, your clients and your competitors? Naming is important. There are consultants who now coach parents-to-be on what to name their infant. Naming is more than important; it is an essential tool that will enable you to be found by the right people. Query any search engine to see who else shares your name. How well does your name and the name of your company translate on a global scale? If you are beginning to build your brand, now is the time to think about tweaking your name in a way that will distinguish it from all the other *John Smiths*.

jellybeans are hell of a lot more memorable than *johns*.

I remember once hearing an anecdote about Barbra Streisand. She wanted to work with the guy who had a *candy-sounding* name. Turns out she was talking about Jellybean Benitez. His association with Streisand catapulted him from the ranks of the up-and-coming to being a star in his own right. Soon *Jellybean Benitez* joined the A-list of such notable producers as Phil Spector, Alan Parsons, Quincy Jones and George Mart.

Now Jellybean's real name is John. Jellybean or John, no matter what name he went by, the man had significant talent as a producer. The question is: *Would Streisand have found him memorable if he had not branded himself as Jellybean?* The defining moment in this man's career came when Streisand asked for a producer whose name sounded like *candy*, not *John*. This doesn't mean that someone named John Benitez would not have gotten the opportunity to work with Streisand. It does mean that jellybeans are a hell of lot more memorable than Johns.

Your name is deeply connected to your brand destiny. From the cradle to the grave, your name will stay with you. No matter what company you work with, or even if you change your job, your occupation, or start a new business, you will take your name and reputation with you. Your name is more than just a name; your name is your complete dossier, your whole persona—a professional brand that will endure for all time. You need to consider building brand equity in your own name by building a professional brand that is, above all else, memorable.

first think about your name.

Celebrities are acutely aware of the brand equity in their own names. They have the distinct advantage of being able to throw a lot of money and resources to create brand extensions— celebrity fragrances, celebrity jeans, celebrity golf tours and celebrity salad dressings. There is no limit to how far celebrity names can be expanded in the marketplace because the budgets can be spectacular.

Individuals need to build brand equity in their own names more than a celebrity does. There is fierce competition vying for market share, to get revenue, to get a job, to get funded, to get a contract or to get a gig. If you are building your career or building a new business, your name needs to be memorable. So what do you do if you are named John? Do you change your name? No, but it does mean that you must embellish and expand your given (legal) name so it is a complete fit with your profession. To wit there are no professional ballet dancers named Bubbles or Buck, lawyers named Tiny Tim or nurses named Evil Kineval.

Your name is a critical component of your brand and it must clearly differentiate who you are and what you do from everyone else, and especially from your competitors. If your name is dreadfully dull and ordinary, and there are a million of you in any city phone directory and on pages upon pages on Google, then my advice to you is to use your most interesting initial, e. g., Franklin D. Roosevelt, John F. Kennedy, and

Thomas A. Edison. It could be an unusual middle name: Ralph Waldo Emerson. You don't have to rely only on a middle initial. It could be your first initial, e.g., J. Walter Thompson, J. Paul Getty, F. Scott Fitzgerald. It could even be two middle initials: the elder George H.W. Bush clearly wanted to be differentiated from his son the *W*.

There is a time when changing your birth name may be the right thing to do. There can be a compelling personal or professional reason to reinvent yourself. I once worked with a woman who had been abandoned by her birth mother and did not want to carry her name, so she created her own name and it helped her to begin building a new brand. Celebrities or creative professionals may want to change their name to transform to a new brand image, such as from a *girl-in-pigtails Norma Jean Baker* to a *sultry blonde starlet named Marilyn Monroe*.

Do not change your name because it is difficult to pronounce. I had a client who was a superb oral surgeon who had a very long and complicated eastern European name. He wanted to change his name to Dr. J. and I advised him against it. This medical doctor had three advanced degrees and was known for his exceptional surgical skill and the ability to undertake the most difficult and complex cases. He was clearly not Dr. J. the basketball player.

If your name is three syllables or longer, people will want to shorten it for two reasons: either they are lazy or they want to make you more diminutive and love you like a pet. Consider complex names that are highly memorable, e.g., Arnold Schwarzenegger, Zbigniew Brzezinski, Gwyneth Paltrow and Isaac Mizrahi. Make people learn how to say your name. Give them a lesson in phonetics. They will remember you.

Having a memorable name that conveys your solid brand identity works to attract the right people, the right clients, the right business partners and the right media. Whatever your name is, you need to understand that it has value. And it is up to you to maximize its value by making it work for you and your core expertise. As a final note… Remember Barbra Streisand? Like a true diva, she always reminded everyone that her name was spelled "Barbra"—without the third "a."

author's note

I am half Italian and half Irish so my name truly defines my ethnicity. I also like its solid rhythm that connotes a certain lyrical quality. There aren't that many women in this world named **Patricia Vaccarino** and I am the only one in PR.

Once you have established your name, you need to build a brand that truly defines you. Instead of thinking about creating a brand that is authentic, forget about authentic. The word *authentic* has been so grossly overused that is now a marketing word *du jour* that essentially means little or nothing. Let's focus on three things. What is real, right and true about you?

self-audit.

Know yourself and your business in order to build your brand accordingly.

People can attach a lot of mystique and voodoo to the concept of brand. Professional branding experts can charge a lot of money to touch brand. **But all brand does is pose a question. The question is: What do you stand for?** It is up to you to answer this question. You must tell your clients and customers what you stand for. So when the time comes to hire someone like you, they remember your name and have an understanding of why they want to work with you.

choose a single identifier.

It's all about you. Each of you has a vocation, a skill set, a talent, a personality and a personal history that makes you unique—it's your Brand DNA. There is no one else out there quite like you. It is your job to find that single brand persona that speaks volumes about who you are and what you do. Begin by choosing a single identifier that describes who you are and what you do—accountant, physician, lawyer, floral arranger, astrologer, publisher, magician, sailboat salesman. Once you have chosen a single identifier, now you need to refine it further. **Identify the three things about yourself that if, for any reason, they were ever taken away from you, you would no longer be who you are.** Choose three descriptive phrases or words that truly describe who you are and what you do. How are you different? Assess who you are and name the three core attributes that define you. How are you different? Be concrete about the attributes. Distinguish yourself from your competitors. Core attributes are the fundamental descriptive words or phrases that describe you. Core attributes can be easily described according to your background, your experiences, your education, your ethnicity, your talents, your unusual skills and hobbies, your athletic achievements, your personality traits and your management style.

core attributes are the building blocks of your brand.

For example, Jean-Claude Steinberg is the CEO of a luxury goods company that focuses on women's accessories and handbags. First, he is French by birth and nationality and graduated from one of the leading French business schools, *École Supérieure de Commerce de Rouen*. Second, Jean-Claude has a strong background in managing companies that produce mass-market brands in food. Third, his management style can be described as consultative, which leads him to rely on the trusted advice of key people in his company. Jean-Claude brings his knowledge and expertise of mass-market brands to the luxury arena. Whether he is leading a conglomerate that sells yogurt

or a fifth-generation Italian luxury company that sells $3,500
handbags, he has a proven track record for slashing costs and
increasing revenue. No matter what company Jean-Claude is
running, his three core attributes remain a constant and define
his brand identity.

niche vs. brand.

Niche should never be confused with brand. A niche defines a
place for you in the market, but it is also very limiting, especially
if you have 500 of your competitors sharing the same niche.
Brand is the way to thoroughly define your core personality.
No one else can have your same brand personality but they
can occupy your niche and compete for the same clients in the
same marketplace.

choose precise visual identifiers.

Visual identifiers speak volumes about who you are and how
you do business. For example, I know a world-class designer
who always wears bow ties. His bow tie is highly symbolic of
his formal nature, his courtly charm, and the long, thoughtful
process he takes to create extraordinary design work for luxury
brands. I am aware of a commercial real estate agent who works
in midtown Manhattan. To define her core personality she relied
on her past service in the Israeli army. To differentiate herself
from other brokers, she wore her army boots to her business
meetings and became utterly unforgettable while she successfully
built her business. Her army boots are not a gimmick. Gimmicks
are not appropriate to establish brand. Instead these boots were
the outward symbol of this woman's courage, strength and discipline. If you want to sell commercial real estate in New York,
you need to demonstrate power. Take Jean-Claude Steinberg:
His visual identifier is his class ring from the French business
school *École Supérieure de Commerce de Rouen.* If you use visual
identifiers to demonstrate your brand persona, send the right

symbolic message that clearly shows the key components of who you are. Be Clever. Be Strong. Be Clear.

a rose by any other name.

The Italian writer Umberto Eco (who borrowed heavily from Shakespeare) noted that a rose called by any other name would still be a rose. Unless it has been genetically altered, every rose has thorns. The rose without thorns lacks its immutable texture and its signature fragrance and is, in a sense, no longer a true rose.

When you are building your own brand, it is all about you, who you really are. It's okay to have thorns, i.e., a weakness or a flaw. In fact, everyone has a major flaw. No one is perfect. Identify your weakness and make it work for you. Position your greatest weakness as a great strength. The number one brand rule about weaknesses or flaws is that they ought to be used as a tool to identify and distinguish you, just so long as they **never, ever** stand in the way of your outstanding performance.

I once knew a very successful Hollywood film editor who had a pronounced stutter. Ironically, people focused very intently on what he was saying while they waited patiently for his words to stammer out. He used stuttering as a way to differentiate himself from all other film editors. If his stuttering had negatively impacted his performance as an editor, he would never have experienced so much success. His greatest weakness was used as a great strength. He was known more for his brilliant ideas and his brilliant editing than he was for his chronic stutter.

brand trust.

What makes you different? Keep in mind that what makes you different should make you appear to be noble, in pursuit of excellence, or full of integrity. While weird and edgy may work for celebrities, these are seldom desirable traits for the business world...unless you're an artist. For a weird or edgy difference to be valuable to your brand, these qualities must still demonstrate value to your customer. Your brand attributes must demonstrate that no matter what, you will always deliver what you have promised to your customer.

You have heard my encouragement for you to identify your own primary three core attributes—the three core attributes that truly identify you as a brand. Now I suggest that you ask your spouse or your mother—the people who know you the best and who live intimately with your flaws—to assess whether the three core attributes speak the truth. No matter how well a person knows you, your three brand attributes should ring clear and true and dominate all other descriptors.

professional vs. private.

There is an increasing blurring of the boundaries between our professional and private selves. The tremendous use of social media has accelerated this blurring of the boundaries. When you build your brand, leave ample room for the good, the bad and the ugly, but here is a word of warning. Don't ever attach anything to your brand that has the potential to come back later to haunt you. Don't post anything in real time or in Internet time that you would not want to be read by your mother, your children, your priest or your rabbi.

The precise reason why Bill Clinton has a more lovable brand than Eliot Spitzer is because Bill is not perfect. Eliot Spitzer feigned perfection and covered up his weakness and prosecuted those who actually shared his same weakness. It's okay to have a weakness or a flaw. In fact, everyone has a major flaw. No one is perfect. Identify your weakness and make it work for you. Position your greatest weakness as a great strength. (More on this in Chapter Eight.)

🎵 pr note

brand warning.

Consider the stunning fall of the governor of New York within the context of understanding the human brand. If only Eliot Spitzer was a little more like Bill Clinton. Even if you're a Republican or a fan of Obama, it's impossible not to like Bill. Bill can get away with a dalliance here or there because it never interferes with his main brand message—he's Bill. Look at Bill's core brand attributes. Bill is Southern. Bill has charisma. Bill is so comfortable with people from all walks of American life that he can easily communicate with and inspire anyone from a coal miner to a Microsoft millionaire. Bill has never pretended to deny the cad-like component of his brand persona. Being an occasional bad boy makes him all the more endearing—more human, sort of like a "Benjamin Franklin." When considering your own brand, don't create a persona that is stiff or artificial and denies some core aspect of who you really are. If you completely whitewash and hide your dark side, you will find yourself lighting a fuse to a powder keg instead of a cigar ;)

brand legacy.

When creating your brand, it is not the time to be lovable or confusing or slow. Assess the language that you use to define who you are and fine-tune it with the precision of a wordsmith. Be Clever. Be Strong. Be Clear. Developing brand equity in your own name is essential for success and will ultimately define how much you are worth financially, professionally, emotionally and spiritually. As always, I want to remind you that personal and professional brands aren't built overnight. Building a brand takes time and perseverance. Using the media as a tool will help to build your brand. You can change your job, and even your career, but you, the brand, will remain for all time. Brand familiarity alone guarantees nothing. It is how you execute your own brand that becomes powerful and memorable, a living legacy. **Be a legend in your own time.**

chapter two 🝔 positioning

connect with your community.
positioning has two faces.

Positioning includes the two opposite spectrums of your brand and poses two very important questions that are linked: **Who are you now? Who do you want to be?** Positioning may have two faces but only one face is shown to world. The face that is shown to the world is **Who do you want to be?** Who you want to be is your vision.

For example, at one time, Robert B. Parker <u>aspired to be</u> a successful mystery writer *who would create* a popular hero named Spenser who would be macho, but lovable and sensitive. **Robert B. Parker knew who he wanted to be. And because he knew clearly who he wanted to be this vision came true.** Robert B. Parker <u>is</u> now a successful mystery writer *who has created* Spenser, a macho, but lovable and sensitive, popular hero.

At the root of the face you will show to the world, you will find your vision statement. It is this vision statement that will dictate the boundaries of your position. **Who do you want to be?**

Your position is really who you are in the process of becoming, i.e., who you want to be. Every aspect of your persona and how you interact with the world must fit the parameters of your position, which is the ultimate vision for your brand. In essence, your positioning stance indicates that have already achieved what you want to become.

The two faces of positioning require you to make certain that *who you want to be dominates and overtakes who you are now* so that there is a single brand vision and a strong brand position.

community-of-interest.

Your positioning can be solid and clear only if you identify your community-of-interest. You must identify everyone in your community-of-interest. Your community-of-interest is everyone who stands to gain value from knowing you. You must include media, current clients, prospective clients, former clients, vendors, service providers, referral sources and rainmakers, your colleagues, your investors, and, believe it or not, your competitors, your friends, your former teachers, your family and even your mother!

For an individual or group to become a part of your community, they should:

- Have a vested interest in knowing you
- Respect you and listen to what you have to say
- Receive value from you
- Know what you stand for
- Have the potential to refer business to you
- Be able to attest to your past performance and rely on your future performance, i.e., your brand integrity

Your community-of-interest is composed of just about everyone you already know and everyone you will want to know. To be vital, your community must be a growing community. You should be constantly meeting new people who stand to gain enrichment from knowing you. With the advent of the Internet, there is no reason to keep your community local; you can expand it to be a global audience. It is your Brand World.

You must continually provide value to your community. To keep your community strong and cohesive you must always ask yourself the following questions. Who are your loyal followers? Who has watched you evolve professionally over time? How do you repay their loyalty? Why are they watching you? Lately, what have you done for them? These questions are a call to action. You must never take the members of your community for granted.

building your community-of-interest.

Once you have established your community-of-interest, how will you focus on building your community? Developing new partners and networking are the obvious answers. (This is discussed in great detail in Chapter Eight.) However, it is important to establish the following priority. **In the new media age, you must use social media and social networking to enlarge your community-of-interest.** Whatever community you have established in the real world should be replicated online in Facebook, Linked-in, Twitter and other highly trafficked social media websites, so you can stay in constant communication with the people in your community. The whole point of using social media is to stay relevant in your community, to keep your communication current, and to keep your conversation alive. So when the time comes to hire someone like you, you are on the top of your community's list.

expert positioning.

Another aspect of your brand positioning has to do with making you an expert in your field. You can create a more focused brand persona by being positioned as an expert in your chosen line of work. So what does it mean to be an expert? According to Wikipedia, *An expert is someone widely recognized as a* *reliable source of <u>knowledge</u>, <u>technique</u>, or skill whose judgment is accorded authority and status by the public or their peers.* I have an additional requirement to add to this definition. An expert is someone who gets paid to practice or provide expertise. There isn't a person among us who does not have a clearly defined expertise about some aspect of life. When it comes to establishing your personal brand, your expertise must be clearly defined and promoted to your community-of-interest. Expert positioning creates a level playing field because your brand is promoted on par with another person who shares your same occupation, but who may actually have stronger credentials and greater experience than you have.

For example, Marc Riddell is a 27-year-old author and self-styled HR consultant. He has an undergraduate degree in business administration, but no advanced degrees. Since graduating from college he had two different jobs; both were with advertising agencies and were relatively short-term. Although he had published a book about the twenty-something work force, his book was self-published and lacked polish, sophistication or powerful testimonials from his colleagues. Yet he was interviewed and quoted as an expert in the *New York Times*, the *Los Angeles Times, Leadership Excellence, The Wall Street Journal*, and the *Washington Business Journal*.

create a new category or name.

Another aspect of expert positioning involves the creation of a uniquely defined expertise. We have already spoken of the rabbi who was a youth and culture expert or the plastic surgeon who specialized in the psychological aspects of cosmetic surgery. In Marc Riddell's case, he positioned himself as an expert in HR issues for the twenty-something workforce. There are many other highly credentialed experts who could have been a source to publications that had instead featured Marc Riddell. The difference is Marc Riddell had consistently promoted his brand and his book, so when journalists were writing stories under deadline, his name was one of the first "experts" to come to mind. Positioning and promoting yourself to the media allows you to become a source—the first person to show up on the media's radar. Positioning and promoting yourself to your community-of-interest allows you to become a first choice—the first person to come to mind for a position, a project or a contract.

brand as a business.

What business are you in? There are some businesses that have great brands, but they're about to go out of business. **Sears.** There are some businesses that have great brands and great business models. **Amazon.** There are luxury brands that spend more money on branding, marketing and PR than they spend on product development and manufacturing. These brands are in the business of making people feel rich and exclusive. **Prada. Chanel.**

There are some brands that you have never heard of because they just believe in business and do not put any effort into developing brand. **Wego.** Owned and run by several generations of the Azrak family and located on the fifth floor of the Empire State Building in New York City, Wego creates private label clones of mass market, well-established brands like a $1.50 look-a-like version of Dove antiperspirant or a $1 version of Johnson and Johnson baby wipes. Wego licenses the rights from Procter and Gamble or Unilever and creates a low-end market for cheap clones. You think you're buying Dove so why pay more for the same item? In the dollar store the clone looks real. The Wego website has been under construction for five years. http://www.wegony.com. Wego doesn't need any web traffic. Wego is in the business of not being a brand, but of making money off of well-established brands. Even not being a brand is still a brand.

identify your brand's community-of-interest.

What kind of brand are you? Are you a Sears, an Amazon, a Prada or a Wego? What business space are you operating in? What changes in the current socio and economic climate are affecting your business? Who are your competitors? Do your competitors thrive because you are in business? Remember how Starbucks, as a disruptive marketer, opened up a whole market space to sell coffee as a luxury beverage? Starbucks prospered enough to create a new market that gave room for the birth of new competitive brands such as Tully's, Peet's Coffee, and SBC. Starbucks also fostered its own healthy competition with these other brands. Even though you are a personal brand, and not a corporate brand like Starbucks, your competitors may still be the source of your greatest strength and your allies and advocates. Either you all stay in business and compete with one another and prosper, or you all go down together.

take a look at the competitive landscape.

How well does your brand resonate in the current economic or political climate? What is going on in your community-of-interest that has a direct impact on your business? Know your target audiences in your community. Connect with your audiences. This does not mean you dilute the integrity of your brand persona and become someone else. It does mean you must adjust your brand so your audience gets what you are all about. For example, MacDonald's didn't leave behind the fast food market, but it did start offering coffee at a much reduced price to compete directly with those purveyors of luxury coffee—Starbucks, Tully's, Peet's Coffee and SBC. Now MacDonald's is the disruptive marketer, the upstart that is responding to the changing needs of the community. You must constantly refine your brand, so that it speaks directly to what your community needs. And keep in mind that those needs are constantly changing.

Sleeping with the enemy. You must not only know your competitors, but you must love them. The scene in *The Godfather* when Don Corleone says, "I hold my friends close to my heart, but I hold my enemies even closer," speaks precisely about the true nature of American business. I speak from the core of my Sicilian heritage when I say *The Godfather* is a great metaphor for American business. Collaborate with your enemy. Sleep with the enemy. Throw cold water on your face and get over it. In the end, it's all about holding your position and making your numbers.

Fred Santoro, an East-Coast-based marketing pro, told me that his startup business was groundbreaking, totally one-of-a-kind. He said he didn't have any competitors. Not one. No enemies? Not one! I knew he had at least a hundred competitors—just in Seattle, Portland, and San Francisco. Imagine what's going on in Chicago, New York, L.A. and Dallas. What's wrong with this guy? He isn't reading. He isn't doing his homework. He's not doing the math. He's not networking. He thinks he is ahead of the curve, but he is really behind the eight ball. If you do not have competitors, then you have not built an effective community-of-interest. You must know your competitors and how to position yourself among them to your best advantage. Then you can use your community-of-interest as a focus group:

- Make certain your brand is clearly defined and positioned.

- Make certain your three main key brand attributes are clearly communicated to your community.

- Check to see if your community-of-interest understands how you are different from your competitors. (Ask some trusted members directly: When someone mentions your name, or the name of your company, what images come to mind?

* Offer your community-of-interest a range of services and products that are priced differently than your competition. (This does not mean you offer lowball prices. It may mean you actually increase your pricing.)

* If you can operate at a lower cost, then pass these savings on to your clients and customers, but make certain that your customers know.

* Offer your community-of-interest services and products that are bundled in unique offerings and package deals.

* One way to gain advantage is to do things differently from your competitors in a way that offers unique value. This can mean offering a different array of services or a combination of services with greater efficiency and better turnaround time.

The strategy behind effective positioning must always take into account the current social, political and economic landscape, your community-of-interest and the competitive landscape. The world population is about to reach seven billion! The sub-prime fallout, the strained credit markets, the rising costs of fossil fuels and food did not happen in a single powerful earthquake. We are seeing a long series of slight tremors that are hardly felt, but afterwards a whole continent will have shifted its location. Some predictions indicate that, after the fallout, China will take the Number One slot for the largest economy and India will vie with the US for the Number Two slot. There is always tremendous opportunity in an economic downturn. How to prepare? What to watch for?

Now is the time for you to implement a strong position for you, your brand and your business. Think about doing business outside of your own comfort zone, your own city and your own nation. Think Global. Think about whether your brand speaks to a local audience as well as it speaks to a global audience. Your brand positioning must be constantly checked, evaluated and improved.

chapter three ✿ perception

expertology—the new reality

What's the point of being good at what you do when no one knows who you are? Did you ever wonder why, even though you have very strong expertise, someone else seems to be getting all of the press coverage? Do you wonder why reporters and producers choose to interview your colleagues or your competitors and they don't interview you? It's not that you don't have the credentials. We know you do. It's just that outside of your small circle of friends, no one seems to know who you are. You just aren't positioning yourself to a larger and higher-quality community-of-interest. **You need to understand that if you do not promote yourself, no one outside of a small circle of friends will know you even exist.**

Paul B. Brown, who covers small business issues in the *New York Times*, featured psychologist Judith Sills in a column he wrote for the February 9, 2008 edition. Paul referenced Judith Sills from an article she wrote in *Psychology Today*. Ms. Sills suggested people become their own brands by being acknowledged as an expert. She wrote that a person's brand "is the professional identity that you create in the mind of others." What was her message? Sills advised that by building your own brand you will stand out or stay employed in the current deteriorating economy. Forget about gestalt therapy, eating disorders, early childhood trauma and obsessive-compulsive disorders; even psychologists are recommending that you build a strong brand.

I recently met with a surgeon who is considered to be one of the top in his field. Aside from his medical degree, he has a specialized master's degree from a top-tier university. He really is an expert. He is a pioneer in heart surgery, a world-renowned expert on open-heart surgery. The surgeon doesn't really want to do publicity but feels as though he ought to. He wants to continue to be perceived for the reality of who he is. He feels that even though he has a thriving practice, other doctors who are not as highly reputable, and do not have his credentials, will overtake the public's perception of who is truly the expert because his competitors have promoted themselves, and he has not.

What we are dealing with is reality and perception. What matters now, more than ever before, is the public's perception of who is an expert. That expert status is carefully crafted and cultivated over time. It does not happen by accident. People are not featured in the media by accident. It takes aggressive PR campaigns to put them there. Essentially what we are dealing with is reality and perception. Perception is now the new reality. And it must be managed.

Lawrence Bullock works for Credit Suisse and has survived three rounds of massive layoffs. His annual salary plus bonus is greater than the gross national income for some third world countries. He once remarked that he has seen a lot of not-so-smart people make huge fortunes and some very smart people make very little money. In his estimation, making money has more to do with having a certain flair for PR instead of just having dumb luck. Some very smart people are clueless when it comes to PR. They don't think they need PR, and in the long run either they don't make money or they don't get the credit for their accomplishments. They are often passed over for opportunities that are given to people who manage their own brand personas. One thing is certain: If the world's perception of you is not closely related to the reality of who you are, then ultimately you will not achieve the highest level of recognition for your own brand persona. You might still make a living, but you will not get the recognition you deserve.

An example of someone who has made a lot of money in his lifetime but still faces a challenge with his brand persona is George Soros, the chairman of Soros Fund Management, best-known as a speculator and a political activist. Soros was recently on tour with his latest book, *The New Paradigm for Financial Markets*, in which he argues that a "superbubble" has developed over the past 25 years and it is now collapsing. Even though Soros made a fortune by doing things such as betting against Britain's currency in 1992 and Thailand's in 1997, more than anything else, he wants to be perceived as an economic philosopher. Since he was a student in 1952, he has been promoting his economic theory, which he calls "reflexivity." And since 1952, legions of academic economists have been dismissing his economic assertions and relegating his theory of reflexivity to the ranting of just another hedge fund manager's "write downs." Despite his ability to make billions, George Soros is still pressing on to repair the wide chasm between how he is perceived by his critics and how he wants to be perceived.

brand control.

Remember Jean-Claude Steinberg? He is the French CEO who came from a mass consumer goods background and now runs a luxury retail conglomerate with a "consultative" management style. Does the world believe that Jean-Claude Steinberg is an excellent leader who has a consistent track record for increasing a company's bottom line? Or is there a gap in the way the world perceives Jean-Claude Steinberg as a brand? Is there the suggestion in the media or in the boardroom that Jean-Claude is not fully effective at running a luxury goods company because his background is in mass-market food? Is there the lingering impression that Jean-Claude is an autocratic leader who has only feigned the art of listening well? As it turns out, Jean-Claude has been given excellent performance reviews for five years in a row. Three years after he took the helm, the company's sales and profits grew even faster than Jean-Claude Steinberg had initially planned. And even during a declining demand for luxury goods, the company recently rose to the 45th position in *Business Week*'s "Top 100 Brands" chart created by _Interbrand_.

Whether you are leading a company, a practice group, a project, a small business, or an organization, your brand leadership style sets the tone for the entire operation. Your brand persona has been enlarged to personify the very face of the business. Consider Jack Welch and GE or Bill Gates and Microsoft or Steve Jobs and Apple. In each case, a powerful brand persona came to signify the core values for the company. So aside from evaluating your own brand persona you must also look at your business. Is your internal brand reality in alignment with the external perception of your brand? Do the people who work with you understand your company's brand, which is made evident in its mission, vision and core values? Do they put these core values into action?

Every professional must decide how they want to be perceived. You must consider whether integrity is needed to be part of your brand. You can't have trust without integrity. You must decide if trust is an important factor in how you do business and how you want to be perceived. You need to think about whether you care about being trusted.

the chasm between reality and perception.

Having a good professional reputation is obviously connected to establishing one's brand persona, but many people don't take the time to nurture and grow their own brands because it requires consistency and hard work. You might want to give yourself an audit. Is the world's perception of who you are in alignment with who you think you are? Go to trusted members in your community-of-interest and ask them to tell you what they think you stand for. We have discussed the two faces of positioning and unifying *who you are* together with *who you are becoming* so that there is a single brand vision and a strong brand position. If there is a chasm between the reality of who you are and how you are perceived, what will you do to bring the perception of who you are into alignment with how you want to be perceived?

bridging the gap between reality and perception.

Bridging the gap between reality and perception means the right stories must be told about you as a brand. Ultimately brands are about people. And we know people in stories they tell. The more stories you have, wrapped around a person, the more insight to the experience of that person there might be. I come to know you as a person professionally. If there is a chasm between the reality of who you are and how you are perceived, then you need to narrow the gap. And even if the reality of who you are is in alignment with the perception of who you are, you still need to manage this perception. No matter what, you need to know which PR tools to use to communicate the right stories about you and your brand.

chapter four ⅋ platform

brand forever. forever u.

The platform is the major building block to develop your ongoing PR campaign. The platform is composed of your key PR messages. Every professional has more than one audience. Remember your community-of-interest includes everyone who stands to gain value from knowing you: media, current clients, prospective clients, former clients, vendors, service providers, referral sources and rainmakers, your colleagues, your investors, your competitors, your friends, your former teachers, and your family.

Each audience may get the same PR message about your brand or they may get slightly modified messages. For example, what I say to the media about you might be slightly different from what I say to one of your competitors. The messaging platform is actually much more than an essential building block in every PR campaign. The platform is also the foundation for every piece of communication that speaks about you, your brand or your business.

Every messaging platform is the basis for any and all content or copy that is written in your business plan, in your marketing, sales and business development materials, in your brochures and direct mail pieces, in your newsletters, press releases, emails, on your website, on the blogs, and most important of all, in any statements you make to the press, and in any of your posts on social media websites.

Before you say or write anything, give yourself a test. Is your communication consistent with your platform? Your platform ensures that anything you say or do will be consistent with your brand: your persona, your position and how you wish to be perceived. In order to aggressively drive your brand forward, what are you going to say to your community-of-interest?

the platform of marilyn langford.

Below are some key messages that were created for a talented graphic designer named Marilyn Langford. Please note how each message is altered ever so slightly to hone in on her different audiences.

To the media: *Marilyn Langford is a designer's designer, a true visionary, whose expertise far surpasses graphic design and can strategically shape and map the development, expansion and evolution of a luxury brand.*

To other designers and colleagues: *Marilyn Langford has created a proprietary process, Creative Mapping™, and works with prestige clients to create all aspects of the visual brand. The Creative Mapping process oversees the development of all the visual components that make up retail products, product launches, product innovation and the full spectrum of luxury goods and services.*

To clients: *Bringing over 17 years of experience to her work, Marilyn Langford excels in imbuing luxury brands with emotions, experiences and shared cultural assumptions that can be extended across all touch points. She creates merchandise that indulges clients and instills them with confidence in their choice. Langford is a designer you can count on to deliver superb work on time and within budget.*

To her friends: *Marilyn Langford is a great person and very successful designer who frequently works with well-known luxury companies. In her spare time, she works on her own art and last year she had her first showing at a gallery in Chelsea.* **To her mother:** *Remember when Marilyn was a kid? Even then she was always into art. Her grade school notebooks were decorated with amazing doodles and sketches. It is no wonder that she went into a field where she gets paid well for her creative talent.*

Any of these messages could be delivered to any of Marilyn Langford's audiences, for they are all consistently communicating the high quality of her work, her innate design talent and her many years of experience as a designer who works with luxury brands. As you can see, it is always to your advantage to have a variety of messages that speak to different audiences, but still communicate the consistency and strength of your brand persona.

what is the foundation of your story?

What is your message? What are you saying to your community? Does your message define you? My recommendation to you is to start by creating one solid general message that will work for every member of your community-of-interest.

Here is a general message for a CPA and certified financial planner that can be communicated to all audiences. *Dennis O'Mahoney has taken his knowledge as a CPA and combined it with his experience as a certified financial planner CFP® to provide a heightened level of service to his clients. He is known among his colleagues as an exceptional financial strategist who provides consistent and long-term value to his clients.*

Assess the language that you use to define who you are and fine-tune it with the precision of a wordsmith. Here is a general message for an internationally renowned artist that can be communicated to every audience. *Antonio Riviera echoes the confluence of Cubism and functionalism, the lightness of being and the strength of form.* His work can be classified as abstract symbolism with some of the figurative aspects of neo-expressionists. His use of neo- expressionism fuels expressionistic fervor, a passion that translates into the sense of touch. On some deep level that you may find inexplicable, Antonio Riviera touches you.

stay away from jargon.

Stay away from jargon and steer clear of words that are over-used, misstated or otherwise characterized as belonging to a popular trend that may have already passed its peak. Trends in language are similar to trends in the marketplace. Don't be the last person to jump into the swimming pool when everyone else is already in the pool and ready to get out. Stay ahead of the curve. When you are the last to get out, you will always take a hit and suffer a loss.

For about ten years many marketers used the word *authenticity* to define the heart and soul of a brand. The new marketing word du jour is *sustainability*. Eliminate clichés and buzz words like "authenticity" and "sustainability" that dominate a marketing trend. Use of this type of language will dilute your message and your brand and will prove you are like everyone else during a time when you need to stand out. Set forth the finest examples of the results that you get for your clients.

self-audit.

As always, we return to the process of self-audit. Know yourself, your brand, and your business in order to craft your message accordingly. Know your target audience(s) and customize your message for each audience. What you say to your potential investors will be slightly different from what you will say to your potential clients. And yet it must be emphasized that if you do not feel as though you have the expertise sufficient to craft different messages, you must create one solid general message that will resonate with all of the audiences in your community.

Here is a strong general message about an up-and-coming fashion designer, which unifies the designer and her work, i.e., bridal gowns as one brand. *It has only been a few years since the work of Magda Milosevic has captivated the bridal industry. Magda Milosevic burst onto the scene and achieved instant fame with her first couture bridal collection, and it is easy to see why: just like the designer herself, Magda Milosevic's bridal gowns are a powerful expression of the magic of fashion and its ability to start anew. Femininity incarnate, mystery personified, flirtatious, voluptuous, and never predictable, a blend of the outrageous and the elegant—Magda Milosevic is the quintessential European woman whose work demands much more than a passing look.*

create your brand promise.

Your messaging does more than describe who you are and what you do. Your messaging is actually a brand promise and tells what you will consistently deliver to your clients, customers and colleagues. Your messaging should set the bar as to how you wish to be perceived. Draft a brand pledge that explains how you will serve your colleagues, employees and clients. Find the right words that express exactly what you can do. Be realistic and direct about what you can do.

Your platform must resonate with your audience. The messages that you craft must speak to your audiences. I recently attended a high-tech conference where the keynote speaker was a celebrated marketing expert who had worked in sectors from high-tech to consumer products. The marketer used case studies featuring Prada, Gucci and Louis Vuitton—all luxury fashion brands. I watched the audience for reaction and saw blank expressions and squirming in squeaky chairs. There was a problem. The audience was composed of wealthy male techies whose idea of fashion was to wear wrinkled khaki pants and color-coordinated socks with their Birkenstocks.

The marketing professional who gave the talk was so intent on extolling his own image and so taken with his own work in luxury fashion that he lost sight of his audience. His platform failed. He didn't have a message except to say that he knew how to market luxury fashion brands. If only he had demonstrated his marketing expertise by using his case studies and insights from the high-tech world. If an experienced marketer can make this mistake, so you can you. When you create your platform, know and understand the needs of your target audience. Connect with your audience. This does not mean that you uproot your platform. It does mean that you must slightly adjust your messaging so your audience gets what you are talking about.

fully execute your brand promise.

Is your word good? The language contained in your messaging platform shows your commitment to live up to your brand promise. Everything you say, or you don't say, should *consistently* live up to the standard you have set forth in your brand promise. Create a message so powerful that it will tell itself. All of your actions, what you do and what you choose not to do, should be consistent with your platform. Remember the French CEO Jean-Claude Steinberg? His colleagues have noted that the door to his office is always open. He frequently consults with employees of all ranks to ask for their opinions on various aspects of the company. Jean-Claude is widely hailed to having a no-nonsense pragmatic approach to problem solving, and he is known to be an excellent listener.

your own brand culture.

The strategy behind smart public relations must always take into account human resources. The two most important "Rs" in business are *PR* and *HR*. Seattle-based branding expert Sean

0'Connor thinks human resources should be renamed *human relations*. I agree. The people who work for you or with you are the evangelists for your brand. These people are your face to the world and they can talk you up or talk you down. They can make or break your business and either undermine or bolster the strength of your brand.

you must lead by establishing your brand in your business.

If you are clear about your messaging, then your brand will become the dominant theme in the culture. Find the right words that express exactly what you can do. Do it. And deliver on time. Your platform should speak volumes, not only about who you are and what you do, but also tell about how well you do it.

Regardless of the industry or sector, I have observed large-cap companies, mid-cap companies, startups, solopreneurs, government agencies, academic institutions and professional firms hiring people to just do a job instead of taking the time to explore whether a new hire really fits within the *"brand culture"* and in particular fits with its mission, vision and core values that are all communicated in its messaging platform.

We have all worked with people who were just good enough to get you beat. Who is doing the minimum to get by? Or maybe their definition of "good" isn't good enough. It is a time to make tough decisions about whom to let go and then to recruit new talent. Who is really an evangelist for your brand and who is not?

No matter the position, top to bottom, from CEOs to receptionists, everyone who works with you is actively engaged in your public relations outreach and is executing your brand platform for the entire world to see. When you have your Rs (*public relations* and *human resources*) in alignment, it is inevitable that the third and most important R of all *(revenue)* will follow.

chapter five 🔉 planning

you are your own business. invest in you.

Professional brands take a minimum of ten years to build. To successfully build your brand, you need to be consistent. To get breakthrough results, you must actively communicate your brand messages over a sustained period of time. The strategy of launching your campaign is tantamount to launching an all-out military offensive and it requires an investment of time and money.

The primary tools you will use for strategic planning include Press, Pitching, Partnering, Performance and Persistence.

Press relations are a critical component of your campaign. There is no single media outlet that will reach your entire community. If you needed to reach the entire population tomorrow, a whole lot of tweeting and posting could happen with immediacy, but many people are still going to get their news from TV, radio, online news sites, print newspapers, late-breaking email alerts, the billboards in Time Square, or by watching the mini-TV screen in an elevator or the back seat of a taxi cab. There is no one certain channel of communication to reach your community, and this reality explains why your ongoing public relations requires strategy, planning and effective communications tools.

know your own brand world.

In order for you to know what tools to use to reach your community, you must know the people in your community. You must know what they read, what they watch, where they go, what events they attend, and who influences them. Your successful brand is based upon your emotional linkage with your community-of-interest: media, current clients, prospective clients, former clients, vendors, service providers, referral sources and rainmakers, your colleagues, your investors, and, believe it or not, your competitors, your friends, your former teachers, and your family.

How do these people feel about you? For you to truly know them, you need to find out all about them.

1. WHO are they?

2. WHAT do they do?

3. WHERE do they hang out?

4. WHY do they need you?

5. HOW do they feel about you…How do they **really** feel about you?

Once you have identified some basic information, such as what they do and where they hang out, you can begin to make a list of the media outlets that will reach them and design a budget to buy advertising, marketing and PR placement. During the next two years, it is time for you to implement a strong public relations outreach for you and your business. It is clear that as a professional, each year, you will put money into your appearance, wardrobe and business entertainment. In addition, you must also plan an annual budget for your own PR campaign. You will need to set aside anywhere from $300 to

$5,000 per month. It all depends on just how much you want to spend to invest in you.

To communicate to your community-of-interest you will need to have a website, a schedule of speaking engagements, a schedule of networking events, memberships in professional organizations, listings on social media websites, a press kit, and marketing collateral which includes brochures, direct mail pieces, and backgrounders that tell about you and your business. These items are all mandatory and are all integral to launch your own ongoing campaign.

There are some communications tools that are optional, such as having your own blog, writing articles for relevant trade magazines, and generating a newsletter. These tools should not be implemented unless you can write well, you can write well *with great frequency*, and you can add value to your community with the topics that you cover in your writing.

In the case of blogging, everyone has already been in that pool and is looking to get out. There is every indication that over 90 percent of existing blogs have been abandoned by their owners. Unless you are a terrific and prolific writer who can create a blog that is on the edge of American innovation and you can give it your undying devotion and attention, you don't stand a chance of getting traffic and gaining traction.

Other visual communications tools include the creation of visumes (90-second video clips that feature you as a talking head) or longer seven- to eight-minute video vignettes that tell a powerful story about you and your business. The other optional tool is podcasting, which, like video, can be placed on your website or launched as content on a multitude of social media sites.

All communications tools, whether they are critical to build your brand persona or are merely an option, must all be checked against your messaging platform to ensure the consistency, integrity and value of your brand.

your face to the world.

No matter what type of business you are in, you have to have a website that clearly communicates what you have to offer. The website is more than your face to the world; it authenticates your business and speaks volumes to your community-of-interest. A strong website coupled with an aggressive public relations program is, by far, the best return on your marketing dollar.

Your website should convey clear and strong messaging about you and your business. Other than paying for placement to boost search relevance on Google, the best way to drive traffic to your website is to get picked up in the media.

Scout around to determine how much you need to put into your website. Do you need to upgrade, redesign, and come up with a fresh new look? Should you explore Search Engine Optimization to improve traffic to your website? Do you want to improve navigation and usability to influence retention for the visitors who come to your website? To increase search relevance, how much do you want to spend on advertising, marketing or PR to potentially increase traffic to your website?

pr note

Linkage. If you don't have a pressroom on your website, get one. When you do get quoted or featured in the media, get the links to those articles posted on your website.

a brand march—the annual plan.

Once you determine your budget, you need to establish priorities for each and every year that you are in business. Each year, set a specific date to review your communications tools. Decide how much time and money you will spend. Establish the priorities of what is needed immediately and what is optional and can be held off for another year. You need to allocate costs (both time and money) to your essential communications tools:

+ Your website

+ A calendar of speaking engagements (you are a profiled speaker)

+ A calendar of networking events (you are an attendee)

+ A calendar of trade shows (you are an exhibitor)

+ Memberships in professional organizations (composed of your potential clients)

+ Your listings and posts on social media websites (which are continually updated)

+ Your press kit (can be used for the media and for business development)

+ Marketing collateral, which includes print brochures, direct mail pieces, and backgrounders that tell about you and your business.

If you cannot create these tools, you need to outsource to the professionals who will create these tools for you. And even if you have some of these tools in place, you will need to annually revisit each item to make updates and to improve content.

You need to think about how you are managing your own time and then budget your work hours accordingly. You must spend one to two hours every week planning your outreach. This does not include the time you must allocate to get projects completed, e.g., to write a new brochure or the time spent interviewing new web designers to redo your website. You must also spend time every day both planning and using the right tools to wage your own public relations campaign.

You must undertake this campaign as if you are going to war. Your "enemies," real or perceived, or your challenges, obstacles, and other barriers to success are much larger than you are and often have much greater financial resources. To stand a chance at winning, you must routinely allocate your own time and resources. This is what you must do to build your brand, your business and remain memorable. There are no shortcuts. Another definition of public relations is business development. And don't ever forget that.

chapter six ❧ press

the world wide web of media.

Media relations is the most crucial part of any PR strategy. It can take companies and individuals to unforeseen heights, create new trends, and build innovative markets. Before you embark on any sort of media relations, you need to understand that the media as an industry is in a state of flux. The transition from the Industrial Age to the Age of Communication is complete. The Old Media has fragmented into the New Media.

People who would have been working in manufacturing 30 years ago are now working in the New Media as reporters, editors, producers and, most notably, as bloggers and social media gurus. Many traditional media outlets, such as the regional newspapers, have gone out of business or have stopped publication in print and only maintain an online presence. Even with the high rate of attrition among all the dying traditional media outlets, there is a whole new wave of media outlets that are starting up. The New Media is creating enormous clutter.

The dissemination of news through *free* social media like Facebook and YouTube has given traditional media outlets some ruthless competition. There is also some pretty compelling evidence to indicate that for some time the big media outlets have been over-leveraged, bloated, and have been expecting unrealistic advertising revenue growth.

mixed-up media.

In the push to grab greater market share, the media is getting mixed-up. With diminishing readerships of traditional print, and diminishing viewers of traditional TV, the old newshounds are expanding into the realm of new media like they invented the turf. Oldster Rupert Murdoch bought YouTube. *Forbes*, who traditionally covers hard business news, now has an online health and beauty editor! And the *New York Times* is doing TV! And just about every media outlet has a Twitter handle and is transmitting instant news briefs in real time.

Overheard and attributed to Marc Andreessen of Ning at the Allen & Company conference in Sun Valley, Idaho, July 2008: "Nondigital businesses are toast… If you have old media, you should sell. If you own newspapers, sell. If you own TV stations, sell. If you own a movie studio, sell."

Marc Andreesen's comment is extreme, sort of a hue and cry to herd a stampede to a quick fire sale in which he may have his own self-interest at stake. Despite Andreesen's alarming call to action, print will live and flourish in the New Media world. Social media will not replace print media any more than computers replaced paper and created paperless offices.

The traditional media outlets, especially print magazines and regional and daily newspapers, are getting beat up right now, but in the next wave, if they can ride it out, they will be fine. Until social media becomes profitable as an industry, it will continue to lose luster and give the traditional media players new opportunity for growth, if only they are tough enough to weather the storm.

There is still a huge global population that wants to read in print and enjoys the portability and visceral feel of a book, a magazine or a newspaper over a mobile device or a Kindle. There are new magazines starting up every day. While we undergo the current media meltdown, it just means the media outlets that had taken on too much debt will be sold. In the future, there will still be printed books and printed media but companies will be leaner, with less overhead, and will require less capitalization to print limited, high-quality editions based on already credible brands like the *New York Times*, *The Wall Street Journal* and *The New Yorker*, and the powerful, well-branded journalists who write for these publications.

🎵 pr note

small media is good media.

Media serving communities-of-interest and niche markets are increasing ad revenue. Some local newspapers serving boomtowns and rural communities are growing. According to Philip Murray of Dirks, Van Essen & Murray, which is the leading merger-and-acquisition firm in the U.S. newspaper industry, "In small markets, newspapers continue to be the dominant ad platform. Prospective buyers are betting that better days lie ahead for a business that sells information, a valuable commodity in any market."

face value and air time.

Self-audit. You also need to take a hard look at yourself to assess whether you are fit for certain types of media. If you write well, you can author bylined articles and become a featured writer or blogger. If you are mediagenic and articulate in front of the camera, then it is possible for you to be an excellent source or expert for TV news. Do you have a wonderful and engaging voice? Then radio and podcasting can be a good outlet. Consider all forms of media: Print, Broadcast (traditional TV and Radio), Internet, Blogging, YouTubing, and Podcasting. You need to assess two major factors: which media will reach your community and which forms of media work best for you—for your look, your voice, your persona, your writing ability, and your quotability.

the *new york times* on air.

Even people who are communications professionals and work with media have a challenge when it comes to assessing whether they are a fit for TV. Deborah Solomon, who has talent in print, asks the most arresting and thought-provoking questions of her subjects profiled in her Sunday *NYT* magazine column. On *Times On Air,* however, a TV program produced, packaged and distributed to weary air travelers on Jet Blue, Ms. Solomon appears on screen as a quasi-anchor or talk show host. Her hair looks good and her wardrobe doesn't clash, but she pokes and pushes her glasses, plays with her hair, performs troublesome tongue gyrations, and has the quirky movements of someone trying to find her small dog while smiling nervously because she does not know where to look to avoid staring directly into the camera. A succession of rapid, jerky jump-cuts makes *Times On Air* look like it has been edited by a first-year NYU film student and reminds us that "All the News Fit to Print" is not good TV.

when looking good is essential, don't assume you will look okay on camera.

If you plan to be on Broadcast (TV) or in a visual media production, invest in the right training. Hire both a media skills training expert and an image consultant. The media skills training expert will teach you what you should say, how to say it and how to move flawlessly on camera. The image consultant will show you what to wear, what to do with your hair and how to make up for the lighting and camera angles. Looks do count. Except when they don't.

what is the best way to reach your potential clients?

How do your clients get news? If you don't know, ask them. Is it from *KING-5 News*, *Parade Magazine*, the *New York Times*, *CNN*, *Daily Candy*? Put together a short list of the media outlets most relevant to your profession and to your clients. Every client I have ever worked with wanted to be on *Oprah* or the *Today Show*. Be realistic. The *Puget Sound Business Journal* or *Entrepreneur* might be a more appropriate placement than *Oprah*. Your potential clients will most likely read business press and are not at home watching *Oprah* at 4 o'clock in the afternoon.

print vs. broadcast.

PR Newswire has an online media directory (Media Atlas) that is competitive to Bacon's, which is the gold standard among media directories. Both of these directories can be found at any municipal public library. These directories now add 50 to 100 new media outlets each business day. These media outlets cover online publications and print publications as well as TV and radio. Please note that this does not include blogs.

I have seen clients get more traffic to their websites as the result of regional daily newspaper coverage than their appearances on national TV. It's the clickability factor. It is easy for a reader to click from a news site to your site. Broadcast is ephemeral and only as good as the time it was transmitted. Print will stay out on the Internet forever. A post on social media will get a blip for a nanosecond or two.

Telling your story to the world is the same as it has always been. Create your press list. You need to precisely identify the media outlets that will reach your current clients and your potential clients. Build your press list according to the type of story and the theme of the story that you want to tell. Old Media, new media, social media, it doesn't matter. What matters is that you get the word out. Use any media to do the job.

press list.

It is essential to include media in your community-of-interest. You must also keep in mind the Number One PR maxim to live by: Good PR is establishing the greatest number of high quality relationships that reach across industries and sectors to get you a return on investment. This means that you should engender as many high quality media contacts as you can.

Keep in mind that media contacts are constantly changing jobs. I recently found a media list that I had put together for a client in 2000. The rate of attrition was about 80 percent—the same as CEOs, only media don't get the same compensation package and signing bonus.

Create a customized press list that will reach your target audiences. Your press list should be a blend of older traditional publications as well as new media startups and social media. Here are some quick tips to get you positioned in the media outlets of your choice.

pr note

what you need to know in the new media world.

1. Research the Internet and make a list of reporters/editors/producers who cover areas (beats) that are significant to you and your business.

2. Follow reporters/editors/producers and research their past coverage. Know their story topics.

3. Note when a reporter/editor/producer moves to a new publication, network, or website.

4. Media are the most receptive to talk to you when they have changed jobs. Send an email, say hello, and tell them what you appreciate about their work.

5. Tell them how you can help now or in the future. Be brief.

6. Pitch the reporter with a topic or story angle that is directly related to his beat. Be very brief.
7. Stay in touch. Check in every month or so. Be really brief.

Add media contacts to your social media communities.
Include social media to your online social media communities. If word-of-mouth is the most effective of all PR tools, then you need to work with people who can passionately communicate your brand's message to the world. **A note of caution:** If media are included in your social media networks, that is all the more reason to make sure every word that comes out of your mouth is consistent with your brand persona and your messaging platform.

press releases.
The press release is dead. Long live the press release!

The all-points-bulletin press release is a relic of the past. Most media outlets prefer a customized story pitch that was created specifically for them. Stories are routinely placed with media by sending an email pitch or calling a reporter on the phone. And yet the press release can still be an effective tool when used correctly.

Press releases convey a wide range of information necessary to generate awareness and raise your image with your key audiences. Topics can include:

- Financial reporting to board members and shareholders
- Financial reporting to Investors
- Documenting events and professional milestones
- Creating content for your website press room

- Announcing new partnership with key industry players
- Announcing new services
- Announcing new product
- Announcing your awards or achievements
- Sponsorship of special events
- Achievement of goals or landmarks
- Completion of a new project
- Personnel announcements (can be major)
- Content of speaking engagements
- Commentary on industry issues and trends
- Acquisition of a strategic partnership
- Acquisition of a new client
- An acquisition and merger

There are occasions when the only point in drafting a press release is to place it on your website for archival purposes and as a way to record some historical event that has had an impact on your brand or your business. The press release is also a great way to create a document that has all of the complete and accurate background information to hand over to the media.

press kits.

You need to have a press kit that exists in print and all of its content can be replicated electronically. An electronic press kit is simply the press kit contents without its presentation folder (press releases, bios, backgrounders, etc., that can be sent to anyone by email). The press kit can be used for much more than only the media. The press kit is a great tool to use for investor relations, business development, and sales and marketing. It can be used as a "leave behind" for your clients and potential clients.

The press kit should make you memorable. Just be certain that whatever you send, it is only a gift or a bribe when appropriate to do so. The contents of your press kit should be part of your messaging and fit with your professional brand image. Don't send any gifts to newspaper reporters or editors. Send expensive gifts to magazine and Internet editors. Send great gifts disguised as press kits to all media.

The bribe. Don't send any gifts to newspaper reporters or editors. Don't offer to buy them a drink or even a cup of coffee at a gas station. According to professional journalistic ethics, this is tantamount to a bribe and is a major faux pas that will keep you off the list.

Gifting. Send expensive gifts to magazine and Internet editors. Magazine editors expect great gifts: jewelry, accessories, gourmet food treats, expensive wine, spa services and theatre tickets. Beauty and fashion magazine editors love new product, especially large samples and free cosmetic services.

The clever Press Kit. A great press kit is focused on its message—it's all about you and your expertise. The clever press kit can be sent to any media contact. For a nutritionist client, we packed her book and her press kit into a box that contained a bushel of apples. "Healthy" apples were part of her brand persona and who except a snake could accuse an apple of being an unethical temptation?

what goes into a basic print press kit?

- Your bio
- Press releases
- News clippings
- Your company or business backgrounder (fact sheet)
- Product backgrounders (fact sheets)
- Book reviews

- Case studies or testimonials (your clients' success stories)
- Articles you have written or have been ghostwritten for you
- Brochures or catalogues that fit the target audience

What else can go into a press kit? The basic contents of any press kit are the same, but other components can be added depending on the industry you are in, the occasion where you are using the press kit (trade shows and symposia) and the specific target audience.

If you're in high-tech or biotech, white papers, analyst reports, summaries of research and clinical trials must be included. If you're in beauty/fashion, a lookbook is a must. A designer or artist might want to include a portfolio. If you're an author, send a signed copy of your latest or greatest book. If you are in a creative field, you can be as creative as you want to be in coming up with an innovative press kit that really speaks to your brand.

pr note

The contents of a basic print press kit will be inserted in a presentation folder. Presentation folders can be printed per your design specifications or the specifications set by your graphic designer. A presentation folder print run can cost anywhere from $500 to $8,000 depending on the ink, paper, folder style and the complexity of the design. You can save costs by purchasing presentation folders in bulk and in your choice of color. You can order labels printed with your name and logo that can be affixed to the folders. Savings are considerable for "labels" and readymade presentation folders.

what goes into the deluxe electronic press kit?

1. Press Releases
2. Latest news and speeches
3. PR team contact information
4. Photos of you, your executives and board members available for download
5. Your bio and the bios of other key executives in your business
6. Low and high-resolution images available for download
7. Streaming video in both Windows Media Player and QuickTime
8. Downloadable broadcast quality video (b-roll, company video)
9. Logo library
10. Image and Video light box function
11. Simultaneous multimedia search capability
12. email registrations by area of interest
13. RSS
14. White papers
15. Service or company backgrounders
16. Analyst reports and summaries
17. Product backgrounders or fact sheets
18. News clippings
19. Book reviews
20. Book excerpts
21. Newsletters

22. Case studies or testimonials (your clients' success stories)

23. Photos of location, events, people

24. Calendar of events and speaking opportunities

25. Links to mutually beneficial websites, blogs and organizations

26. Articles you have written or have been ghostwritten for you

27. Brochures or catalogues that fit the occasion and the target audience

28. DVDs, CDs and podcasts.

29. Suggested reading (articles, excerpts and peer review publications)

how to use your press kit.

The contents of your press kit should be available in print and electronically. The key is to know when to use either format. In routine communication with the media, it is easy and cost-effective to send the contents of the press kit by email. It is advisable to send the more deluxe print press kits when you are conducting a major campaign such as a product launch or the release of a new book. Another occasion for the print press kit is when you are going on a press or analyst tour and you need to bring along background material to your interview.

pr note

Press kits are expensive to produce, so they should be used sparingly and only when—in your estimation—the recipient will appreciate receiving the full press kit and be able to use it to your advantage—for example, as background information for your interview.

♪ pr note

Use Media to Exercise Your Brand. Even though the media has become highly fragmented, there is no greater credibility than getting authentic news coverage. Utilize every facet of media. There is more media than ever and these media outlets range from the equivalent of 3-pound dumbbells to the bench press. You can write for many media outlets and blogs or get them to cover you or your business. Outreach to the media is a discipline. There are no shortcuts. Spend one to two hours every week responding to media requests.

you are an expert. become a media source.

You can create a more focused brand persona by positioning yourself as an expert in your field. Every time you are quoted or featured in the press you have created greater brand prestige for you and for your business. The primary objective of positioning yourself as an expert is to build brand equity in your name. Instead of relying on PR people to provide their clients as sources, there is a growing trend for the media to want to build their own rolodex and deal directly with a source or an expert. So put yourself out there now.

- Track reporters who cover news relevant to you and your business.
- Send each reporter an email with your bio. Introduce yourself.
- Compliment their work and tell them why.
- Open a dialogue. Build a relationship.
- Stay in touch by email or phone on a monthly basis.
- Send the reporter information relevant to their beat.

- Send the reporter other experts who are relevant to their beat.

- Comment on their new stories even if you did not participate.

- If you see a story in the news that speaks to your expertise, then immediately email or call the journalist and let her know you are available for interview.

press relations—The hidden rules.

There are some hidden rules about working with the media that you should know. Most journalists will not tell you the rules because they don't have the time, budget or temperament. If you don't abide by the rules, you won't get placed, or if you do get placed, the information about you may turn out to be all wrong—wrong name, wrong title, or the wrong words-out-of-your-mouth.

There are now many ways to learn what journalists are searching for. If you have access to a media switchboard service, then you will routinely receive requests posted by the media.

pr note

who are you? you're not fred!

I have received feedback from journalists that they have received lengthy expert opinions or loaded commentaries and the "expert" just signed off as "Fred." No full name. No occupation. No business name. Just Fred.

This is okay if you really are Fred—the iconic and freakish six-year-old with anger management issues, who began posting videos to YouTube and ended up with a cult following. But most of us are not Fred; we are professionals who need to present ourselves in a way that is memorable, compelling and fast.

So when you are responding to a media query that has been posted by a journalist, there are a few things that you need to know:

1. Meet the deadline. Some deadlines are a few days and some are only a couple of hours. Respond ASAP. Many reporters will turn OFF their queries after they have received enough responses.

2. Put the subject of the query in the subject line of your email.

3. In your email, immediately identify yourself, your expertise and the name of your business in one sentence. Be memorable in how your describe yourself. You should also include your bio or a summary of your credentials toward the end of the email along with your contact information. How are you different from everyone else who could be answering this query?

4. Answer the journalist's query with a direct response in two or three sentences. Don't just say you are available to talk by phone. (I've seen two extreme responses, from *War and Peace* to telling the reporter you are available to talk about your response by phone. Both responses are inadequate. Be memorable in your response. Make it stand out but keep it brief. Hold on to *War and Peace* for your blog.

5. Do *not* send journalists to your blog or to your website by firing off an email that states you have had success with the requested topic, but only providing information such as "please see my Web site," "read my book," or "read my article." You will end up in the "delete" file.

6. Don't send attachments unless this information is requested.

7. Write the precise answer to their question and keep it brief. Give a good sound bite—you don't have to serve up the entire dish, but just enough to pique their interest.

8. Do not switch your pitch. Do not "pitch" the journalist with what you really want to talk about in lieu of providing a direct response to their query. This is sure death.

9. Remember, whatever you say, or whatever you write, can be used out of context. It can also stay on the Internet for a long time. Choose your words wisely. There is a much lower risk of being misquoted when your response is in writing.

10. Follow up once more just before deadline to ask journalists if they have what they need. This kind of conscientious follow-up will ensure a higher likelihood of placement. Be gracious and offer to continue to be a source. Ask journalists if they will send you an email when the story goes live (to print, online or on-air.)

♪ **pr note**

tracking media placement.

If you are featured on radio or TV or quoted in an article, no matter what kind of media placement you get, you must follow up with the media source to capture your press coverage and add it to your website. It can also be leveraged as a promotional tool to send to your clients and colleagues.

---

brand control.

It is okay to say "no" to a press opportunity. No need to say "no comment," just pass on the media opportunity altogether. There are bad media placements that can actually harm your brand. Here are two examples:

Five fat ladies on the job. The management team of a high-tech company was composed of all women—five overweight women to be precise. The press photographer, acting like an art director, placed the women sitting around a lunchroom table with a huge platter of doughnuts and an oversized coffee pot. The photo in a major newspaper made these women look like they were in a quilting bee instead of looking like five smart, powerful women running a spin-off company for Hewlett Packard.

The CEO lost in the crowd. A CEO accepted an opportunity to be interviewed on CNN during prime time. The CEO sent email to thousands of his colleagues asking them to watch him on CNN. The interview was allegedly about the state of the economy, but the news brief was a cattle call, a town hall, a roundup of everyday people, and the CEO was never identified at all. The CEO's role, his business and even his name were excluded from the interview. Some of the others on the bench were introduced as a postal clerk and an office worker. This positioning seriously weakened the CEO's brand as a person who exercised good judgment and leadership. Even though he was not identified on the air, we knew who he was because he had sent out a mass announcement!

key questions to ask a journalist who wants to interview you.

Never accept a media interview just to gain exposure. You must always learn the scope of the interview and the context for your brand positioning.

- ✦ What is the story about?
- ✦ What questions will you be asked?
- ✦ Who else is being interviewed?
- ✦ Do you need to provide supporting material, i.e., a press kit?

- When will the story run/air?
- Will you verify the facts in the interview?

Press tours.

Setting up your own press and analyst tour will allow you to meet with key journalists up close and personal. Face-to-face meetings are always the best way to develop high quality, long-term relationships. But before you place that first call to schedule a meeting, make sure that you have the right talking points. You should be able to discuss your expertise articulately, succinctly and with great confidence. You must be able to provide the latest information about your industry or expertise. It is ideal if you have news to announce, such as the launch of a new product, company, or an opinion that is timely and relevant to an emerging trend.

Research your editors and producers. You don't necessarily need to access the databases used by PR professionals. Internet research can cover a lot of ground and provide you with most journalists' recent articles and programs. You should be able to see how long the journalist has covered a beat and get a handle on his writing style, pet peeves and specific areas of coverage.

Your presentation needs to be an excellent conversation. You should lay the groundwork by putting together a pitch that covers all of the salient points of your presentation. A well thought-out presentation is essential. You must make certain that the content of this presentation is consistent with the key messages in your platform and your overall brand persona. Remember, your presentation is not formal. Your presentation is actually a conversation that is seeded with your key messages about your expertise and your opinions as a thought leader in your industry.

Self-audit. You must assess the strength of your presentation skills and if they are mediocre or inadequate, it is time to get training from a professional. Effective communication requires training and practice.

One word of warning. Before you pitch a story, put yourself in the position of the editor. The editor's office is actually a small cubicle in a "sick" building that was built during a time when "green" was only a color. It's 5 pm and 400 *unread* emails are in the editor's inbox. He has 16 urgent voice-mails waiting for response. Eighty faxed press releases sit in his fax machine. The editor doesn't even have the satisfaction of smoking strong cigarettes or drinking cheap bourbon. What are you going to say to this editor that is timely, relevant and compelling?

Press Kit + research. You should include relevant research that you have compiled and have it ready to go in a document that must be inserted in your press kit.

Verify your meetings. Journalists are always under deadline and you can get bumped due to a late-breaking story. Close to the day of the meeting and again on the actual day of the meeting, call to verify your appointment. Always provide your phone number in case there is a schedule change.

Post meeting + wrap. Note if the journalist had questions during your interview that you needed to answer at a later time. You should follow up and provide this information as soon as time permits and while the interview is still fresh. Now is the time to ask the journalist if she needs any additional information, so you can follow up. And don't forget to send a thank you note. Keep in mind that this is the beginning of a long and mutually beneficial relationship.

Getting picked up in the press is still the most effective and credible way to build awareness for your brand. You need to make a very important assessment about how often you will make an outreach to the press. In the New Media world only one thing is certain: Your media relations outreach should be consistent and focus on both traditional media outlets as well as social media. And all of your communication to the media must be checked against your messaging platform to ensure the consistency, integrity and value of your brand.

chapter seven 🕭 pitching

pitching—the art of telling the story.

What story will you tell? What is your pitch? And I mean what is your story? What is the story you tell about who you are and what you do, and what you can do for your clients? Can you tell this story to me or to anyone else in thirty seconds or less?

We have established that ultimately brands are about people. And we know people in the stories they tell. That is, the more stories that you have, wrapped around you as a person, the more insight there is in coming to know you as a person professionally.

- You need to tell a good story.
- Give the finest examples of your results.
- Show powerful testimonials or case studies.
- Let your clients do the talking and tell your story.

case studies.

Your clients are the best measure of your success. Use credible case studies to tell your story. Case studies are the stories about what you did for your clients. Get your clients to talk about you or and why they like working with you. Get them to talk about what you did for them. This is how you "*Show, don't tell.*" Your client's case study can be used in many different ways:

- The underlying story in your pitch to the media.
- Crafted as a story and placed on your website.
- Used as content in a press release.
- A case study can be a standalone profile in your press kit.
- A case study can be used as a story in your newsletter.
- Posted on blogs.
- Your client can be interviewed at an event or on video/podcast.

No one likes bad or boring communication. In down economies carpetbaggers and snake oil salesmen are everywhere. Invitations to get-rich-quick seminars, how to flip a home in ten days, and free steak dinners for free portfolio check-ups—the same old stuff abounds. If you don't like hearing tawdry tales, then don't tell them either. Be very careful about any stories that you create for you and for your business. Make certain your stories provide value to your community and resonate with your messaging platform.

consider the bald eagle and the turkey.

There are many stories to tell that do not need to include your clients' case studies. In this case, pitching means coming up with a story that will sell. Consider the bald eagle and the turkey. The bald eagle was chosen over the turkey to become America's national bird because the eagle looks regal, flies at a higher altitude and has a better brand story—it's a rare bird. The turkey might be smarter than an eagle, but there is something very demeaning to having a national bird that can be fattened, stuffed and eaten on a public holiday. I think that if the turkey had a good PR program, it might be found on the back of the dollar bill instead of on your holiday table.

You need to think about what is essential and powerful about your story. Are you telling the story of the lean bald eagle or a plump turkey? Does your pitch suck? When professional PR people put information out there, it doesn't just automatically get picked up by the media. Not just *anything* becomes news. Every time PR professionals pitch the media, they have to put together a story. There can be four elements to a story: the hook, the spin, the heart and the soul. You can place a story with just a hook and the spin, but a truly great story has all four elements, the hook, the spin, the heart and the soul.

Hook is the angle that reeled you in and got your attention. It is the headline grabber and what you see in the newspapers every day. State your most exciting news in as few words as possible.

Spin is the art of telling the story. Every story needs characters. People. Animals. Animated characters. Good guys. Bad guys. The location. Conflict. Climax. Resolution. The ending. As the story evolved, what kept your attention?

Heart. How do the characters connect with their audience? What do the characters have in common with the audience? Does the audience empathize with the characters in the story? What emotions does the story conjure? Do people care? Why do they care?

Soul. This is the most challenging aspect of a story. Is the story rich enough in emotional content to connect with any human being? Does the story have universal appeal? Does the story make a difference in someone's life?

♪♪ 🎵**pr note**

Never Let the Facts Get in the Way of a Good Story.
There is no room for hype or BS, but we need to be realistic
about the state of the media as an industry. They need to
make sales. To increase advertising revenue, they need to
increase the size of their audiences. To sustain an increase
in eyeballs, they need to tell stories that get attention.

yellow journalism.

According to Wikipedia, "Yellow journalism is journalism that
downplays legitimate news in favor of eye-catching headlines
that sell more newspapers. It may feature exaggerations of news
events, scandal-mongering, sensationalism, or unprofessional
practices by news media organizations or journalists." To media
professionals, yellow journalism used to be a derogatory slur,
but in the New Media World, with few exceptions, yellow journalism is the practice *de rigueur.*

Even media baron Rupert Murdoch, chairman of the News
Corporation, is spectacularly astute at telling ailing regional
newspapers how to fix themselves. "Just produce better papers,
papers that people want to read. Stop having people write articles
to win Pulitzer Prizes. Give people what they want to read and
make it interesting." *WSJ June 9, 2008*

psychological pimping.

Psychological pimping means that your story must establish
an emotional connection with your community. Your story
must make people feel, or, if they do not feel, they still see and
understand how they should feel. Another professional once
told me that a story should talk about features and benefits. I
thought, What planet are you on? Telling a good story is about
getting people to feel, to connect, to empathize and ultimately
to buy what you have to sell.

🎵 pr note

If it's sensational, but true, tell it. Tell it now. (So long as the story is consistent with your brand persona!) Brands are about people making personal, emotional connections from one person to another. We come to know and experience people through the stories they tell or the stories told about them. The boundaries between Marketing and PR and Advertising have blurred, and this blurring has created a new media monster that is hungry for good stories that are clever, powerful and rich. Whether it's *pay to play* (you pay for the advertising) or *pay to get played* (you pay a PR professional to get your news coverage), stories need to be good enough and smart enough to get the spotlight focused on you.

your pitch sucks. ask any turkey.

Now you want to know if your pitch is any good. There is help for the wannabe pitch person. Check out *Your Pitch Sucks* http://www.yourpitchsucks.com/about.html. Submit your draft pitch to PR experts for review. They will let you know if your pitch is up to par and, if it's not, they offer suggestions to hone your new craft.

Pitch new clients. Pitch old clients on new services and products. Pitch media. Pitch partners. A pitch is more than a good story. A pitch is good conversation.

Pitching is not a sales pitch. Pitching is ongoing communication (regularly scheduled outreach) to your community-of-interest by phone, newsletter, blogging, email, posting on Facebook, Linked-in, Twitter, and face-to-face meetings. Pitching is dialogue. It is staying in touch with your community-of-interest. Simply put, pitching is the art of ongoing conversation. Pitching is the unraveling of a story over time. Remember Scheherazade? If you are trying to save your own head, you will tell the greatest story of your life.

chapter eight ❧ partners

partners—the full range of networking.

We have established that good PR is having the greatest number of high quality relationships that reach across industries and sectors to get you a return on investment. It is an understatement to say that you need to network. You need to bring your networking to a higher level. This means you must develop strategic partners, so you can give and receive extra value from your partnerships by working together to maximize your PR and business development activities. By working together with partners, each person can augment credibility, awareness and the impact they make on your entire community-of-interest.

you need to network in four primary ways:

- Events—Attend targeted events. Network at groups and organizations.
- Events—Get speaking opportunities.
- Events—Create your own events with partners.
- Social media—Expand your community-of-interest.

your calendar of events.

When you create your annual plan and budget, also establish a calendar of events for the year. Make a list of organizations of all sizes and types to assess which groups have the greatest potential for you to develop business. Your calendar should be composed of two types of events: events you will attend as a participant and events where you have been asked to give a presentation or a keynote address. Both types of events add value to your brand persona. Your calendar should only include events and conferences that have the strongest potential to support your networking and business development efforts. The calendar should leave room for local events. Allow some flexibility for events that just pop up and seem worthy of your exploration.

walk the talk.

Attending targeted events can make a difference. Every month you should be attending several networking events: social events, trade shows, roundtable discussions, product launches, user conferences, think tanks and large conferences.

Several times a year, you should attend large conferences and trade shows that are relevant to you or to your business. It is not necessary to exhibit your business at trade shows. You can gain maximum networking opportunities just by attending, walking the show and talking to the exhibitors and participants.

Every event that you attend should be well organized, publicized in key media and give you plenty of time to meet and greet the attendees.

speaking opportunities.

One of the most effective ways to gain high quality exposure for you and your brand is by speaking before a group of people. Aside from achieving a high level of credibility among the attendees, many events have media who cover the event, increasing the likelihood for you to get news coverage. Here are some require-ments for getting speaking opportunities.

- Audit the regional and national landscape for speaking opportunities that fit with your expertise.

- Rank potential speaking opportunities according to pres-tige, importance, and compensation given to speaker.

- Rank events according to "quotable" opportunities—most likely to be covered by media.

- Identify the point person for the organization or event.

- Conduct outreach to the point person to book your speaking engagements.

- Draft a dossier composed of your speaker's bio, photo, talking points or speaking topics, and benefits to the audience.

- Transmit bios, photos and any other collateral required to book speaker engagements.

- Follow up to confirm the speaking engagement.

- Ensure your bio is posted on the event or organiza-tion website.

- Ensure logistical details such as finalizing location, speaking date, size of audience, and contact info for any media who will be covering the event.

- Contact attending media to set time for an interview during the event.

be real. be known.

Seize any opportunity you are given to speak before an audience. You have the immediate potential to increase the number and quality of your clients and partners. The notoriety can help to retain existing clients and expand your business network. The publicity that you get can be leveraged to make more revenue through additional speaking, workshops and publishing articles. There is the added probability of driving traffic to your website, blog, etc. Your speaking appearances can create the public expectation of higher fees, allowing you to charge more for your services. Finally the public exposure opens doors to otherwise inaccessible individuals and opportunities. There is no substitute for face-to-face introductions that would not ordinarily have happened had they not occurred at a public event.

partnering for events.

You can always create your own events, so you can give a workshop or webinar to talk about your expertise as long as it creates value for your attendees. These events should charge an admission fee. Otherwise they will not be valued by potential participants. The best events create strategic partnerships or buddy programs with other professionals who complement what you do. You can provide much more value to participants by producing a comprehensive program that covers multiple but interrelated subject areas such as a tax accountant, an estate planning lawyer, and a certified financial planner; or an organic food expert, an organic wine wholesaler, and a chef. Professionals have the ability to co-brand and, most importantly, can share their own business contacts with one another. With this extra marketing power, several professionals who partner can put on events that are lively, informative and educational for a fraction of the cost because you are all sharing one budget.

the exit strategy in networking.

As a PR professional, I have made a career out of attending networking events. Even though I smile through the photo opps, I consider networking to be hard work that requires focus and discipline. Some events are free, like crashing local Rotary luncheons, and some are expensive—Greg Furman's Luxury

Marketing Council has an annual membership price tag of
$7,500, plus the cost of the monthly program meetings.
I have belonged to general business networking groups such
as FirstDegreeNYC or the gender- specific group American
Business Women's Association, as well as highly specialized
trade associations like the Washington Biotech and Biomedical
Association (WBBA) or even the ethnic-centric, Seattle-based
Italian Club, which is so far removed from New York City that
no one in the group has ever uttered the word *Mafia*.
Networking events are not about making friends. Networking events are an opportunity for you to make as many viable
business contacts as possible. When you're doing business, your
time is your most valuable asset. You owe it to yourself to be a
ruthless networker.

In all of my networking activity, one maxim I have come
to know: If you are networking for business, no matter how
expensive or how *free* it is to attend the event, there are certain types of people who will always be there, and you must
quickly identify them, because for one reason or another they
are not capable of ever giving you business. You must have an
exit strategy in place to quickly extricate yourself from someone
who will only waste your time.

Jenny from the block. Whether you grew up in the Bronx,
on the Upper East Side of Manhattan or in the suburbs of Seattle,
"Jenny" will greet you with icy suspicion. Jenny does not want
to know you because you are not part of her tribe. Jennies come
in all sizes, shapes and flavors and they can even be boys. Jenny
has made a lifetime commitment of staying inside her comfort
zone and associates only with people whom she has known
since preschool.

For example, Jenny the magazine lifestyle editor told me
she did not have to network and meet new people because
her family grew up in Seattle, and everyone she knew went to
the U-Dub (University of Washington) and she already knew

everyone she needed to know. Ditching Jenny requires extra-special effort. She lingers around and makes fun chit-chat so you can bathe in her golden light. To get rid of Jenny you must do something big. You must get physical. You must drop to the ground, then rise with your hands outstretched in the air and tell her you are doing the Seattle WAVE because you want to fit in. You have confirmed her worst suspicions about outsiders. She will excuse herself and leave.

The Delivery Boy has a job, and he's wearing a nice suit, but his hair is visibly thick with hair gel and even though it is late in the day, he reeks of Axe body spray. He's not sure what he really does in his job, but he can say the job title quite well as he presses his damp business card into your hand. You can tell he's not the kind of person who takes initiative—he tells you he was told to attend this networking event. He's subordinate in all respects—without an opinion, without a goal and completely lacking in raw ambition. He has no power because he does not want the burden of responsibility. The delivery boy can't even deliver a message. It's too much work. Shake his hand and move on. He will be relieved. He wants to go home early.

The Naked Swordsman is the consummate salesman, a guy's guy. He thinks he's slick, but he's so busy talking he cannot hear a word you say. If you start to tell a story, he will quickly interrupt you and top your story with his own. He will not give you an opening to come back to your story. He will not let you talk at all. He thinks he is a gifted communicator. He does not recognize himself to be a poor listener. Name dropper—he will drop names and tell you who he knows and promise introduc-tions—except most of the names he drops are your competitors. This guy cannot refer you business because he will never give you an opening to talk. He burns with the all consuming pas-sion of the thoroughly self-absorbed. Douse this fire quickly. Spill your drink a little and break away for a napkin.

Hamlet is in love with himself. He is the ultimate narcissist. And even though she is from a different tragic play, his female counterpart is **Lady MacBeth**. Both are immaculately groomed and well branded: sophisticated and quite charming. They even have their own branded language. He does not meet someone new. He has an "encounter." Even if she grew up in Wenatchee, she speaks with a slight British affectation. Both are beautiful to look at and, let's face it, they know how to get your attention and keep you so mesmerized that it is impossible to look away. Hamlets and Lady MacBeths have a powerful shtick to keep you focused exclusively on them: He does not know who he wants to be when he grows up. She describes her current dilemma in great bloody detail. Will you help them to explore their own turbulent life existence?

Most Hamlets and Lady Macbeths are successful—they always have a job or a business. It is not as though they are unemployable. But they are not going to do anything for you, or for anyone. To get rid of Hamlet or Lady MacBeth, you must do the unthinkable; you must divert attention to yourself. Take out your compact, open your mirror, look at your own reflection and smile, or better yet, pick your teeth. Do whatever it takes.

The Spitter does not have to eat or have a drink in his hand to spit. The Spitter is a drone. He is usually very intelligent about his areas of expertise, but completely lacking in business intelligence. He cannot offer you any business. He really does not understand business. He really does not know what he is doing at a networking event. He just knows that he *should* be with people. Unlike Hamlet and Lady MacBeth, the Spitter is not inherently narcissistic. He is simply clueless. It does not occur to him for an instant that you might not want to hear him talk about the latest nuances in molecular biology because you are a member of the human species. The problem is, sooner or later, he will spit. The anxiety of waiting for the moment of the spitting is truly agonizing. He will spit. Trust me. And when that moment comes, you must put your hand to your spittle-laden cheek and say, "Look, it's raining outside, I must go. Now."

networking guidelines.

The following statement should always be operative: **Good PR is establishing the greatest number of high quality relationships that reach across industries and sectors to get you a return on investment.** Remember to allow extra time for a person when you feel that there is a solid business connection, some spark that indicates that you have the potential for an ongoing business relationship. A connection is established when you have had a dynamic conversation, and in less than five minutes, you have both immediately identified precise ways you can be mutually beneficial to one another. Trust your intuition. You feel that you can do business with this person because you are both clearly focused on what you want to achieve. Here are some guidelines to help you during networking events:

1. Wear a nametag that identifies both your name and your company.

2. Always have plenty of business cards. (Even if you don't have a job, be certain to have business cards with your name and contact info.

3. Every business gathering breaks into small groups that can be easily navigated. Be certain to visit every group.

4. Offer your hand and introduce yourself and the name of your company. If your company is not a recognizable brand, you will be asked what you do.

5. Be prepared to state succinctly in under 20 seconds who you are and what you do. Make certain that how you describe what you do is clearly different from others who have the same occupation. For example, I might

say, "Hi, I'm Patricia Vaccarino. I'm a PR person and I specialize in representing individuals—professionals who want to build brand equity in their own names."

6. Hand out your business cards to each person in the group and collect as many as you can.

7. Spend no more than five minutes with each group. Leave as soon as you have either collected a card or have made introductions with everyone in the group.

8. Allow extra time for a person when there is a "connection," some spark that indicates you will have an ongoing business relationship.

9. Right after the event, make a note of the date and occasion on each business card then triage the business cards between the drones and the connections.

10. Take ten minutes to update your social media networks with your new connections!

social media—expand your community-of-interest.

The network that you have in real life needs to be replicated online so when the need arises you can communicate quickly to your community-of-interest. The easiest way to track your new partners is through social media. Use Linked-in, Facebook and Twitter to connect with other professionals. Use these tools to communicate with current clients and potential new clients. Communicate at least once a week—not more, not less. A word of warning: Overdo this and you stand the chance of being de-friended, de-listed or even blocked. Join professional groups and trade associations online even more than you join groups in person. It takes less time, costs less money and, most importantly, the network that you build online should be vetted and utilized as a tool for business development. Social media sets the stage for an actual face-to-face meeting.

don't be fooled by the increasing blur between the professional and personal brand.

What you say on social media can make a long-lasting impression about you and your brand. Those of you who know me, professionally or personally, know that I don't have a tendency to run at the mouth. I prefer to choose my words very deliberately. It's a personality trait that is at the core of my brand persona as a public relations professional. On many occasions, I am required to keep information confidential about my clients, including past clients. There are some secrets I am foresworn never to tell anyone. I have good reason to keep my mouth shut. My favorite Sicilian proverb goes something like this: *One who speaks little makes mistakes. Imagine the one who speaks a lot.*

Since I have been using social media, I have heard my "friends" tell me in great detail about their colonoscopies, teeth pulled, dead dogs, flatulence, adult acne, marital breakups, battles with mental illnesses and drinking problems. I've read lots of bad poetry written by people who are so full of themselves that they do not know that they lack the requisite writing talent to *even think* about writing poetry.

In the world of social media, the one time I was really perplexed was when I knew a "friend" who was desperately seeking a job. He was supporting a large family, had run out of employment insurance and had been forced to go on welfare. With dramatic flair, he reported on Facebook that in his last interview he didn't get the job, but he didn't really want that job anyway!

It's just dumb for anyone who really needs a job to announce to his professional world that he wasted an employer's time in a job interview, especially when he might be talking in real time to his next future employer on Facebook.

don't be stupid.

People are saying things online that they probably would never say to anyone face to face. With social media, you can be vapid, boring, and annoying with alarming frequency. You can say the mundane things that you would only say to a spouse who completes your sentences after you have been married for 30 years. As long as you do not make a negative comment about ethnicity, race or religion, you can be as stupid as you want to be. The funny thing about posting something incredibly stupid is that you will always find someone who responds and "likes" what you said, proving that you can always find someone to be even more stupid than you have been. With so many friends posting at the same time in real time, there is a growing tendency for people who are intent on sharing their real selves to cross the line and behave in a way that is narcissistic.

what will become of your brand chatter?

Instead of seeing authentic selves, we are seeing people say and behave in ways that are excessively confessional, as if they are talking to a therapist instead of to their colleagues, acquaintances, family and "friends." Baring it all on social media seems to be without consequence, but it's not. What will become of your brand chatter? Where will your digital footprints appear in the future? The CEO of an executive search firm recently told me that he was very surprised about the questionable material he finds online about potential job candidates. He is amazed that professionals allow their friends and family members to post unflattering photos and comments for the entire world to see. In the long run, this information can seriously harm your brand persona.

There is an increasing blurring of the lines between what is personal and what is business. This doesn't mean that social media should be used as therapy to expose what we do not want to know about you or anyone else—unless we are getting paid $200 an hour to listen. We all have a dark or dysfunctional side to our private selves. We would not be human if we did not make mistakes and have fatal flaws. But some things are best kept as closely held secrets.

Anyone of Sicilian heritage can attest that Sicilians are a funny people when it comes to talking too much. And I don't mean "funny" in the humorous sense. I mean *funny like peculiar*. I knew one person with the name of *Vaccarino* who was whacked, and his manner of death indicated that he talked too much. He had violated *Omerta, the Sicilian code of silence.*

what do you stand for professionally and personally?

Social media gives professionals the profound opportunity to present themselves in an intriguing and interesting way. With social media you have the tools available to create greater meaning and clarity for yourself and for your own community. You can show your value system and your powerful thinking by sharing ideas and information that can add a richer dimension to all of our lives. We can reveal the back story of how we live in a way that is controlled, thoughtful and enhances our professional lives. But before you pull the trigger and post, you must always put your brand chatter to a test and ask: What do you stand for, professionally and personally?

Remember *The Godfather*? The dominant brand attribute exhibited by Vito Corleone is he didn't talk too much. A gesture with his hand, a raised eyebrow, and the smallest simple physical movements were great evidence of his brand strength. What he didn't say was sometimes more important than what he actually did say. And when he did speak, the room grew deathly quiet; Everyone gave him their rapt attention and listened. Even if iPhones had been around, no one would have been checking their messages. When using social media, it's not a bad idea to be strategic and to think like a clever Sicilian. *Put the lid on your big mouth. What you say on social media can make a lasting impression about you and your professional brand for years to come.*

Your brand speak on social media. A few dumb posts, silly private photos and seriously loutish or bitter opinions can cause long-term damage to your brand. Serious brand damage can affect your sales, your clients, your potential for new business and your overall revenue. Always keep in mind that your social media "friends" are not really friends at all. They are colleagues, competitors, clients and partners.

Brand persona. Humanize your brand by revealing things about yourself that are consistent with your brand platform. You can show some personal details about your real life, friends, family and hobbies, but keep these personal details in line and consistent with your overall brand. This isn't a place to talk about your eating disorders, your credit woes, your crack habit, or your ex-wives (all three of them.) Keep your sins and your personal failings to yourself.

Advocate for your brand. Social media is a bridge to deeply connect you with your community. Here is a place where you can provide relevant, useful information. Whatever your expertise, you can share valuable insights with people who want to learn more from you about what you do. But don't be a drone. Make sure you are sharing useful, insightful information.

Brand articulation. Insight into how you think about your core values, your business philosophies and the world around you will create greater clarity about who you are and how you manage your life. Use social media to articulate your brand integrity. Talk about what matters to you but make certain what matters to you can also have a larger impact on the community as a whole. This is a place to discuss your philanthropy or the charities you support. It is here that you have the opportunity to show leadership and gain support for the projects and organizations that are making the making the world a better place.

social media—professional vs. private.

To fully build your community-of-interest in the New Media Age, you must use social media and social networking. Whatever community you have established in the real world should be replicated online so you can stay in communication with the people in your community. And even though it appears that on social media there is an increasing blurring of the boundaries between our professional and private selves, don't be fooled. Fundamentally, people do not change. They make business decisions on the basis of how they perceive your credibility and integrity. You must be your own best judge of you and your brand and ensure that your social chatter is consistent with your brand platform. The whole point of using social media is to stay relevant in your community, to keep your communication current, and to keep your conversation alive.

chapter nine 🎵 performance

brand penetration—the new metrics of fame.

How do you know when your brand is so powerful that it is "capturing territory" while you sleep? Here is the test: Your brand is powerful when others have expanded your brand to include things that you have *not done* and that you have *not said*, but they are entirely plausible because they are consistent with your brand persona.

For example, I know of a very talented and internationally celebrated designer who does the movie title graphics for many of the feature films released by Paramount or Warner Brothers. His name and work is so often identified with Hollywood that even major films he has not worked on are often attributed to be his work. And other designers have been known to emulate his style to get projects that our more famous designer has declined to work on.

pr note

brand ear.

To keep your brand in shape, have a keen brand ear. Keep your ear to the ground. Maintain many different sources for valuable information. Brand sources are people who come from all professions and have a wide range of talent, experience and multiple forms of intelligence. Don't just listen to your colleagues and friends. Go outside of your immediate community and your comfort zone. You must have unconventional sources of information to get a different frame of reference. Cross-check and compare information among a variety of different sources to keep your brand fine-tuned and sharp.

the fork in the road.

One of the hardest decisions is knowing when to pull the plug on a project or a campaign. If you have reached a fork in the road, it is often difficult to assess whether you should press on and persevere or pull the plug to minimize your losses. Here is a set of guidelines to help you make that decision.

1. Your services are not filling a need in the marketplace.

2. There is a huge glut of your same type of services that are being offered.

3. There are reports that the experience of working with you is awful.

4. Your brand is in the wrong place at the wrong time.

5. Your brand is not clear. No one understands what you do.

6. Your brand is not known. No one knows about you or what you do.

if your brand is not gaining traction, then you need to go back and reassess everything.

This criterion might be an oversimplification, but it will help you to honestly assess your brand when it does not seem to be gaining momentum. If your services are not filling a market need, then you need to get an accurate read by assessing the overall market to determine if there is a legitimate need for your services. If there are reports that the experience of working with you is awful, then you need to immediately do damage control. If the reports are untrue, then you need to manage perception. If they are true, then you need to fix the problem so it does not happen again, and then manage perception. If you are in the wrong place at the wrong time, then you need to pull the plug. None of these suggestions are set in stone. If no one understands what you do or no one knows what you do, then you need to stay the course and continue to build awareness for you and your brand. The evidence of any one of these six factors means that you need to go back to the beginning to audit everything about your brand and your business.

brand momentum.

What does it look like when your brand is being executed properly? Sometimes you are making tremendous strides but you are only seeing the evidence of success in small, incremental results. This is a strong signal that you must persevere! Keep in mind that successful brands are not built overnight. It takes a minimum of ten years to gain lasting recognition for your brand. Here are a few metrics to indicate that you are getting results.

- Increase of new clients.
- Increase in higher quality clients.
- Increase in revenue.
- Increased book or product sales.

- Increase in the number of your speaking engagements.
- Media come to you as a source.
- Increasing ability to raise capital.
- Increase in strategic partnerships.
- Increase in high quality business relationships.
- Increase in traffic to your website.

your name in the news.

Some people believe that good PR should only be about getting as many placements as possible in the media. Not to undermine the value of press mentions, but getting ink is only one component of a successful PR program. It is important to keep in mind that your primary mission is to develop the greatest number of high quality relationships.

Press placement is only the first step. What good is it to get media attention if you do not use it as a tool for business development? If you receive media placement, you must capture your press coverage and leverage it by adding it to your website and using it as a promotional tool to send to your community-of-interest by posting it on social media.

brand value.

Another determinant of your brand success is how well your business is living up to your brand platform. Is your internal PR in alignment with your external PR? Do the people who work with you understand your company's mission, vision and core values? Do they put these core values into action?

your clients are your success stories.

Your clients' successes are your success. It is one thing to have clients, but it is quite another to get the types of clients who bring out the best in you and enable you to work at your highest level of performance. Here are some key attributes of your successful clients.

- Your clients want prestige and recognition.
- Your clients are good at what they do.
- Your clients have something powerful to say.
- Your clients are highly motivated to build awareness.
- Your clients are collaborative and together you work hard to achieve landmark goals.
- Your clients will play an active role in self-promotion.
- Your clients are already successful in their own fields.
- Your clients care about making the world a better place.

control your brand.

If you aren't on top of your own brand-building, then you can be passed over, forgotten or your brand can run out of control and lose its value, i.e., its equity. Staying on top of your brand means you must be an aggressive strategic thinker and constantly position yourself in the way that you want to be perceived. It is just not possible to create a strong professional brand without exerting strategy and a high degree of intuitive intelligence. How your brand is perceived by others is visceral—a gut reaction to you. Be clear about who you are so that you always arrive in the right place at the right time.

chapter ten ✿ persistence

now for the final p in *pr for people*.

It's related to PR, but it is also sort of a personality trait and it requires discipline. It's called Persistence. What's the point of being good at what you do when no one knows who you are? Persistence means never give up.

Kudos to Kazumi Izaki. The 45-year-old mother of two has become Japan's oldest professional boxer after passing the license test of the Japanese Boxing Commission. Under JBC rules, the applicants for a license must be under 32, but Ms. Izaki, a former aerobics instructor, was given permission to apply because she had previously won a Japanese title. Ms. Izaki, who has daughters age 21 and 14, laced up her first pair of boxing gloves in 2001. Citing the reason for her success, Kazumi Izaki told reporters, "I wanted to show my children that if you give up, you're washed up."

brand fitness:

Can you be physically fit and ignore the integration of healthy habits or regular exercise or proper nutrition? The same is true for Marketing & PR and Advertising. You need to implement a strategic program that integrates Marketing & PR and Advertising to build lasting brand equity in your own name. When I train people to do media relations, I tell them *to keep going until they are told to go away, and "no" only means "no today."* Here are some core elements of brand fitness:

- You deliver.
- You don't stop.
- You are focused.
- You are relentless.
- You are visionary.
- You are able to spot trends before someone else.
- You are able to move quickly on new opportunities.

stay relevant.

Do you want to be remembered for who you are and what you do? PR can help build awareness for your professional name and help build your business, but it is hard work and it does require unstoppable focus. The most important thing for you to explore is the following concept: stay relevant. Stay on people's radar. Professionals must build a strong brand, so that they are memorable. So when the time comes to hire someone like you, I remember your name and what you do and why I would want to work with you. It means that the next time your potential clients are looking for a realtor, an insurance provider, an accountant or a banker, an artist or an actor, you are on the top of their list. Stay relevant, and as always, keep your communication current. Keep your conversation alive. And don't forget to pick up the phone and call too!

pr note

Persona, Positioning, Perception, Platform, Planning, Press, Pitching, Partnering, Performance and Persistence—All of these pieces together help to create your brand where the whole is greater than the sum of its parts so that your message of who you are and what you do can break through the clutter.

final chapter ♪ a note about the pr practitioner

shameless and unabashed self-promotion.

Maybe you already have the innate talent and know how to pitch a great story naturally. You don't have to be a PR professional to have great PR skills. Look at Barack Obama or Angelina Jolie. Let's see if you already think like a PR professional.

♪ pr note

be your own pr person, or just think like one.

1. You know how to pose for cameras.
2. At an event you naturally gravitate to the cameras.
3. You know how to speak in sound bites.
4. You know all the issues relevant to your cause.
5. You align yourself with high-profile worthy causes.
6. You create photo opps to show your social, political or business positioning.
7. You know the names of the top five journalists who cover your expertise.

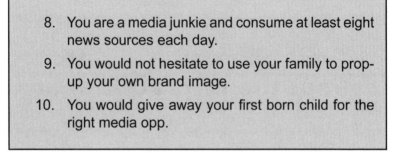

8. You are a media junkie and consume at least eight news sources each day.

9. You would not hesitate to use your family to prop-up your own brand image.

10. You would give away your first born child for the right media opp.

the hidden rules about working with pr people.

We all know that good PR is essential to the growth and viability of any business or any individual. I invite you to evaluate what makes a good PR professional. Some business people think good PR is simply sending out press releases to a press list and then they or their company becomes instantly famous. Others know PR is very complicated, requires intense focus, persistence, dedication, time, money, and its strategy is tantamount to an all out military offensive that is meant to win a war.

There are some hidden rules about working with PR people that you should know. Most PR professionals will not tell you the rules because they are afraid that if they do, they will not get you to be a client. I disagree, because when you don't abide by the rules, I can't do my best work. And if I can't do our best work, then I don't want to work with you.

hiring a pr person.

You have been busy. Maybe your business has grown to the point that you no longer have the time to do your own PR. The time has come to delegate the management of your persona to a professional PR person.

Whether you are retaining a full-service agency or a solo consultant, the same rules apply. These suggestions might shock you, but it is important to tell you the truth so you can manage your resources wisely.

how to manage your pr person on a monthly basis.

1. Stay in close communication with your PR person by phone and email.

2. At the beginning of each month, ask for a schedule of deliverables. The schedule is what he will do to implement a successful program for that month.

3. Review the schedule and make any changes needed so it is clear what the scope of PR duties will be for the month.

4. Make certain the monthly deliverables are consistent with the long-term goal of the PR program and the PR contract.

5. Make adjustments to the long-term goal of the PR program that reflect what is going in your industry or in the current political or economic landscape.

6. At the close of each month, review the deliverables and get a complete update on what has been accomplished to date and what will roll over until the next month.

7. No one knows your business as well as you do. Make certain your PR person is well-informed.

8. No one knows PR as well as your PR professional. Make certain your PR person has made you well-informed so you can make good business decisions.

pr collaboration.

A PR professional can only be successful when there is close cooperation with the client. Give the PR person whatever she needs and get it to her quickly. If she needs to interview you, or your clients, or colleagues, give her the time and attention to get the job done. Get her any needed written collateral material or recaps of past work. The longer you wait, the more inefficient you have made your PR person. Don't delegate unnecessary administrative tasks to your PR firm—it is a time drain and will steal away time spent on the more critical elements of the program.

the pr power of a genuine story.

Understand the power of a real story and understand how a real story is different from a non-story or a so-so story. Some clients think if they hiccup softly, it's news. Understand that your version of what is newsworthy may not really be real news at all. Your PR person knows how to come up with a good story. And when you come up with a good story, your PR person will run with it. Rely on your PR person's judgment. She knows the landscape and what stories are viable in the current state of the media.

pr truth.

PR professionals have the talent, skills and experience to craft great stories. PR professionals are paid well for this expertise. It is a major faux pas to lie. Tell the truth. You need to give your PR person all of the correct information so he can be effective on your behalf. Withholding vital information is the equivalent to going to a doctor to get a diagnosis when you have withheld disclosing half of the symptoms or what you believe to be the true cause of your illness. If you don't trust your PR person to keep confidentiality, then there is a simple solution. Have him sign a non-disclosure agreement. But tell the truth. If all the cards are not out on the table, no one can plan and execute an effective PR campaign.

pay your pr person on time.

Most PR deals are monthly retainer deals. When you pay slow, or you are habitually late with your payments, PR people are slow to work on your account. As long as you are under contract, your PR firm will hit all your deadlines *just like a law firm* but if you pay slow, they will slow down the workload. The reason for the work slowdown? PR people are paid for their service—the time they actually spend servicing your account. Slow, late or non-payment is theft of professional service that cannot be recovered.

pr incentives.

Don't ask your PR professional to render professional service without payment. In lieu of cash PR Professionals are routinely offered trade and barter agreements or stock options. Some of the gifts offered include works of art, cosmetic services, spa services, gourmet treats, event tickets, and free restaurant and bar tabs, which are fine as incentives but not considered payment-in-full for professional services. Cash is the best incentive. Pay the person what she is worth. More importantly, stick to the financial terms of the contract that you have negotiated with your PR person.

♪ pr note

Do not ask for deliverables that are not in the scope of service without negotiating a new contract or understanding that you will be charged for extra time (billable hours). This is the rule but there is a major exception. See PR loyalty.

pr loyalty.

PR professionals pride longevity in their client relationships and will spend extra hours working for clients who have demonstrated long-term loyalty and have consistently paid promptly. Over the course of years of service, retainer fees will not be increased and the long-term client can expect great service for much lower than the current market rate.

pr intellectual property.

Don't ask your PR firm for its proprietary lists of influencers, investors, or media. Your PR person will always give you direct access to specific individuals when it is the right thing to do for both the client and the PR professional's rolodex of resources. But don't ask for a well-documented core dump. It's a deal breaker.

the real pr deal.

Do not feign charisma, charm or likeability. Getting the PR person to like you is not essential to ensure greater success in the campaign. Success is contingent on a whole array of external factors. As long as you pay on time, your PR person will perform to peak capacity.

pr note

The PR person is not your friend except on Facebook. Now genuine friendships do emerge from business relationships, but they are the exception, not the rule. A PR person/client relationship is only productive so long as the PR person continues to offer you benefit.

about the author

Patricia Vaccarino, Managing Partner, Xanthus Communications and *pr for people*.

Patricia Vaccarino has over 20 years of experience working with a wide range of national and international clients, in all areas of public relations: managing worldwide campaigns for global companies and developing strategy for small companies, startup ventures, non-profits, foundations, and individuals. She is especially well known for her talents in strategic planning, knowledge of international communications, coordination of teams based in multiple locations, and creativity. Ms. Vaccarino now owns her own public relations firm, Xanthus Communications, and specializes in PR for individuals who are experts in their respective fields. Many of her clients are listed on http://www.xanthuscom.com. In addition, Ms. Vaccarino currently represents over 150 individuals, many of whom can be viewed on http://www.prforpeople.com.

Ms. Vaccarino has a distinguished public relations record behind her before founding Xanthus Communications. She worked as the director of business development for Girvin Strategic Branding & Design, which is now one of Xanthus' clients. Ms. Vaccarino also worked for the University of Washington as a public information specialist working with research scientists on AIDS, Genomics, and bio-defense initiatives.

Adding to her credentials, Ms. Vaccarino served as the Director of Public Relations for 360 Powered Corporation, which developed groundbreaking search technology for the Internet. Ms. Vaccarino was also a founding member and Vice President of Communications at PublishingOnline. She helped build PublishingOnline from start-up obscurity to ranking fourth among top online book sites.

Ms. Vaccarino graduated with honors from the University of Rhode Island, and also has advanced education from the University of Puget Sound School of Law (now Seattle University School of Law). Also an accomplished author, Ms. Vaccarino has written several books and is an avid storyteller. She has also written award-winning film scripts, press materials, articles, speeches, Web content, and marketing collateral. Her clients have been consistently quoted or featured in all forms of media ranging from top-tier outlets such as the New York Times, the Wall Street Journal, Forbes, Fortune, Crain's, MSNBC, and the Today Show to regional media such as The Seattle Times, The Chicago Tribune, The Miami Herald, and the Pittsburgh Post-Gazette.

About Xanthus Communications LLC

Founded in 2003 by its managing partner Patricia Vaccarino, Xanthus Communications is a boutique PR firm with large firm capabilities that is based in Seattle and in New York. The company has two full-time permanent staff members, five independent contractors and is expanding. We launched *pr for people* in 2008 to house our many experts and to make them attractive and accessible to the media. We also offer the full range of traditional public relations services as well as technologically sophisticated channels of communication. For more information, please visit http://www.xanthuscom.com or http://www.prforpeople.com.